U0693639

杭州Discovery
再西湖

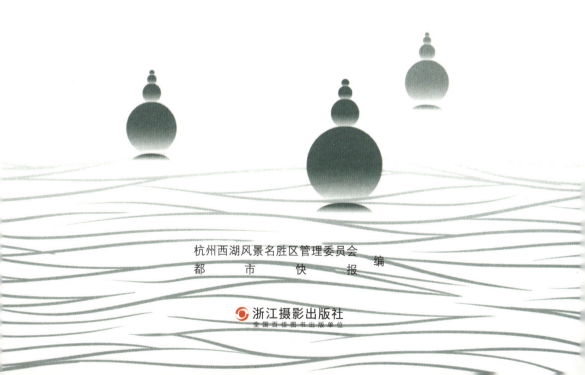

杭州西湖风景名胜区管理委员会
都　市　快　报　编

浙江摄影出版社
全国百佳图书出版单位

总 策 划：孙国方

主　　编：林　琳　何　蕾

项目统筹：倪志华　潘沧桑　何　岚

撰　　稿：余夕雯　斯金叶

摄　　影：陈中秋

翻　　译：高　乾　朱越峰

Master planner: Sun Guofang

Editors-in-chief: Lin Lin and He Lei

Project coordinator: Ni Zhihua,Pan Cangsang and He Lan

Contributor: Yu Xiwen and Si Jinye

Photography: Chen Zhongqiu

Translators: Gao Qian and Zhu Yuefeng

前言

　　杭州，因湖而名，倚湖而兴。

　　西湖，是中国历史最久、影响最大的文化名湖，是古往今来人们心驰神往的风景名胜，是自然与人文完美结合的世界文化遗产。

　　西湖景致自然秀美，饱含人文灵气。在杭州人眼里，西湖就好比是这座城市的"魂灵儿"，一有空就要去逛逛。

　　一年四季，西湖风光各异。春天喝杯鲜嫩嫩的龙井新茶，夏天望一眼满湖荷花，秋天闻着桂花香登高爬山，冬天当然要去断桥赏雪、孤山探梅。

　　一日四时，西湖妙趣不同。早晨去白堤、苏堤、杨公堤跑一圈，下午坐船从乌龟潭钻进浴鹄湾，傍晚一定要去湖滨看看落日，深夜就坐在长椅上静赏一湖月光。

　　"西湖天下景，游者无愚贤。"西湖的美景之所以雅俗共赏、老少咸宜，其实正是因为西湖文化的博大精深、兼容并蓄。由此衍生的景点也多如繁星，各美其美。在近 60 平方千米的景区范围内，除了著名的西湖十景外，还分布着数百处公园景点、文保单位和历史建筑。

　　西湖美景数不尽，西湖故事说不完。因此，对西湖不了解的游客，经常会选择困难，往往是走马观花，浅尝辄止，难以领略西湖文化的精髓。

　　如今的我们，该如何走进西湖呢？答案就在这本《杭州Discovery·再西湖》里。

　　这是继 2023 年《杭州 Discovery·西湖》出版后的又一本"西湖深度游指南"。

　　书中不仅有大家耳熟能详的景点，也有尚待挖掘追寻的秘境，图文并茂，视角独特，可以带你重新去认识、去寻找西湖的湖山佳处和人文底蕴。

　　我们对西湖始终保持好奇之心和探索之意，关注她四季流转的绮丽风景，更在意她富有韵味的文化魅力。这本书，或许会成为我们发现西湖、读懂西湖、更爱西湖的一个理由。

Hangzhou owes its fame and prosperity to a lake.

West Lake, the most influential, time-honored, and culturally celebrated lake, boasts many must-see tourist attractions and has long been a world cultural heritage, representing a perfect hybrid of natural and man-made sceneries.

The views of West Lake are natural and magnificent, in possession of outstanding humanistic value. In the eyes of Hangzhouers, the lake resembles the spirit of the city and will haunt somewhere when at liberty.

Its scenery varies as the seasons alternate. In spring, you will be rewarded with a chance to enjoy a cup of fresh and tender Longjing Tea; in summer, you can feast your eyes on a lakeful of lotus flowers; in autumn, you can go hiking while bathing in the air permeated with the sweet scent of Osmanthus; in winter you can admire the snow on Duanqiao Bridge and the plum blossom on Gushan Hill.

Its spectacular view differs at different times of day. In the morning, you can jog along Baidi Causeway, Sudi Causeway and Yanggong Causeway, and enjoy the sights on the ways; in the afternoon you can cruise from Turtle Pond to Yuhu Bay; at dusk you can watch a sunset by the lakeside; and at night you can take pleasure in admiring the moonlit lake on a lakeside bench.

As Su Dongpo wrote, "West Lake boasts a world-famous lakescape; any sightseer can have their fill of it, regardless of wit." In fact, thanks to the profundity and inclusiveness of the culture that has grown along West Lake, the sights of West Lake suit both refined and popular tastes and appeal to all tourists, old and young. Therefore, a myriad of distinctively picturesque attractions has been developed around the lake. In addition to the renowned "Ten Sights of West Lake", the West Lake scenic area, stretching over around 60 square kilometers, is scattered with hundreds of scenic parks, historical and cultural sites protected at the national level, and buildings with significant historical value.

Words fail to describe the beauty of West Lake and tell local tales. Newcomers are faced with a dilemma in choosing the suitable places for sightseeing and often end up making a hurried and cursory tour without capturing the essence of the West Lake culture.

So how to make an in-depth tour of West Lake? The answer can also be found in this unique *Hangzhou: A Re-Discovery Tour of West Lake*.

It serves as a new roadmap for seasoned visitors of West Lake, following the publication of *Hangzhou: A Discovery Tour of West Lake*.

This tourbook, featured by an extraordinary perspective, vivid descriptions and high-quality pictures, provides an overview of must-see scenic spots and a first-person exploration of undiscovered mythic places, thus taking you on a journey to revisit the best lakescapes and re-admire the cultural richness of West Lake.

We have always been curious about West Lake, and keen on exploring it and especially giving our minds to its seasonally-changing enchanting views and the lingering charm of its culture. This book will likely give us a good reason why we should re-discover, re-understand, and re-love West Lake.

宝石山顶俯瞰西湖白堤、断桥、锦带桥
Panoramic View from the Top of Baoshi Hill: Baidi
Causeway, Duanqiao Bridge, and Jindai Bridge

西湖白堤，桃红柳绿，春意盎然
All-Embracing Spring Scenery at Baidi Causeway: Blossoming Peach Trees and Verdant Willows

白堤是谁修的？
这个问题白居易也曾问过

每年三月，都是西湖白堤的高光时刻。红桃如雾、绿柳如烟，很多人印象里西湖春天最经典的景色就是这样的。

你可能无数次走过白堤，却不一定真正了解它。

2024年年初，《咬文嚼字》编辑部发布了2023年十大语文差错，其中第7条是"误称白居易修建'白堤'"。

西湖最著名的三堤是白堤、苏堤、杨公堤。苏堤由苏东坡所修，杨公堤为杨孟瑛主持修建，唯有白堤的修建者一直是个谜。但可以肯定的是，白堤的修建与白居易无关。

"绿杨阴里白沙堤"，白居易诗里的"白沙堤"就是白堤，而白居易也曾好奇是谁修的这条堤。

白堤犹如西湖中的一条锦带，春季，翩翩柳丝泛绿，朵朵桃颜带笑，是一年四季里最值得打卡的时候。

游白堤，步行是最佳的"打开方式"。整条堤全长987米，宽33米，横贯在湖面上，将西湖自然地分成里湖、外湖。堤上两边，各种着一行杨柳和碧桃。"间株杨柳间株桃"，成了白堤春天最有名的特色景观。

春天的白堤桃红柳绿；到了夏天，里湖荷花正好，"接天莲叶无穷碧，映日荷花别样红"；秋天，北山街两侧的悬铃木青黄相间，白堤是最佳观赏点；冬天，一到雪花飞舞，断桥残雪让西湖的诗意又增添了许多。

除了桃柳，连白堤上一年四季常绿的小草也常常能美得上新闻。

为了留住绿意，每年秋冬季，白堤绿化带里的小草都会重新播种一次，专业说法叫草坪复绿，也叫复播。春夏季，白堤草坪上的小草品种是中华结缕草，它耐热却不耐寒，是一种暖季型草。到了深秋，天一冷它就开始枯黄了，影响白堤美观。这时候，就要复播，接班的是不怕冷的冷季型草，叫黑麦草。

黑麦草能够在冬天正常生长，可到了来年春天，地底下的中华结缕草种子开始重新发芽，黑麦草就要"交班"了。中华结缕草和黑麦草交替"轮班"，才使得白堤草坪一年四季始终保持绿油油的状态。这哪里是在种小草？种下去的分明是西湖的浪漫和温暖！

许多人以为白堤是白居易修建的，事实上，西湖历史上，的确有过一条"白公堤"，但此堤并非现在的白堤。

公元822年，白居易出任杭州刺史，那时的他已经年过半百。白居易对杭州这座城市一直有一种亲切感，年幼时，他曾跟随父亲在杭州小住过一段时间，对这座江南名城的山水诗意念念不忘。

实际上，白居易这次在杭州做父母官不到两年时间，但他在西湖和杭州的发展历史上却是一个极其关键的人物。除了为杭州写下《钱塘湖春行》《杭州春望》等著名诗歌外，他还是一名为民干实事的"优秀干部"，不仅修筑西湖堤防，还疏浚六井。

对于西湖，白居易曾在任上启动过一项大工程——他在上湖（即今西湖）和下湖之间修建了一条堤坝。堤坝建成以后，把湖水尽量蓄在上湖，让杭州的千顷良田有足够的水灌溉，城里的百姓有水可以饮用。

白居易不想通过增加赋税来解决修堤所需的钱粮，修堤可以，但不能增加百姓负担。于是，他一方面发动民间力量，以提供餐食的形式招募工人；另一方面，他捐出部分俸禄，并到杭州的各个寺庙化缘。

公元823年，筑堤工程终于开工。在他离任前的两个月，即唐长庆四年

（824）三月，这条湖堤终于筑成。他为此写了《钱塘湖石记》，刻石于湖畔，为后人留下了西湖治水的经验和故事。

白居易修筑的这条堤坝，蜿蜒在西湖的东北，位置在旧日钱塘门外的石函桥至武林门外，被称为"白公堤"，和白堤仅一字之差。《新唐书·白居易传》《西湖游览志》对此堤均有记载。

"未能抛得杭州去，一半勾留是此湖。"相比另一位"老市长"苏东坡，白居易在杭州待的时间不长，但同样留下了不朽的功绩。对杭州的深厚感情，白居易写在了诗词之中，多年以后，他那首《忆江南》，让无数人对杭州心驰神往："江南好，风景旧曾谙。日出江花红胜火，春来江水绿如蓝。能不忆江南？"

在历史变迁中，杭州的地理环境早已改变，这条"白公堤"现已无迹可寻。

那今天的白堤是谁修筑的？这个问题白居易也问过。

日常工作之外，白居易最爱逛"绿杨阴里白沙堤"，这条白沙堤，就是现在的白堤。见多识广的诗人，一边沉迷于白堤上的美景，一边也在问"谁开湖寺西南路"。也就是说，白堤早于白居易来杭州之前就已经存在了。

历史上，白堤"谁开"之谜，有很多人考证过，但都无法自圆其说。有古籍记载，唐懿宗咸通二年（861），杭州刺史崔彦曾为阻钱江潮水涌入杭城，筑沙河塘时开了白堤。但其实他来杭州的时间比白居易还要晚30多年，白堤不可能是他修建的。

杭州水利史专家阙维民通过文献考证与科学考察，在《钱塘湖白堤与西湖白堤》里揭示出白堤形成的真正原因。

西湖形成之前，水流绕行孤山南北两侧时，因为摩擦力等缘故，流速逐渐变慢。当水流在孤山东头重新汇合时，泥沙就沉积下来。这种沉积，又把汇合点不断地向前推进。时间长了，沿着水流汇合的方向，一条沙堤堆积出来。白堤的人工填土始于西湖与钱塘江隔绝、成为淡水湖之后，大致在唐大历年间（766—779）。

由此可见，今天的白堤形成大致可分为两个时期：前期钱塘湖白堤是自然堤，形成于距今2500年至唐初；后期西湖白堤是由浚湖时的淤泥堆积而成的人工堤，形成于唐中期以后。两者在时间上前后相继，在堆积层中上下互衔。

历史上，白堤曾在元代坍塌败落，直到明万历十七年（1589）才得以重新修筑，并建锦带桥、垂露亭。清雍正二年（1724），为了疏浚西湖，白堤开启加高、加宽工程，并进行了花木桃柳的补植工作。

大抵是从清代起，为了纪念白居易对杭州和西湖的贡献，世人逐渐将"白沙堤"称为白堤。拥有独一无二美景的白堤，自此又多了一重含义。白居易修建白堤的说法虽然是个误会，但千载过后，唯有民心不易。杨柳依依，山色空蒙，每一位从白堤走过的人，又怎么会忘记他。

除了自然好风光，白堤上还有许多人文景观。"乱花渐欲迷人眼，浅草才能没马蹄"的白堤，在白居易之后，还留下过无数文人墨客的身影。苏东坡看雨的望湖楼就在白堤旁，明代张岱的《湖心亭看雪》里所提到的"长堤一痕"亦是白堤。

在白堤上，不得不提的还有断桥。在白堤一端的断桥，仿佛是西湖的门户，踏上断桥就跨进了西湖的大门，因此常常被作为西湖的标志。西湖十景里的"断桥残雪"，是十景中最难见到的景观之一，因为杭州的冬天虽然寒冷，却很少下雪。

还有一个冷知识：很久以前的断桥，是姓"段"的。直到现在，断桥拱顶石上方的栏板外侧还刻有"段家桥"三个字。

有关段家桥的来历，杭州历史学会副会长仲向平曾这样解释："很早的时候，交通不够便利，一座山、一条河、一座桥，取名都是各取各的，也许造桥的时候西湖边住的居民是以段姓为主，也有可能是姓段的居民捐建的桥。叫的人多了，后边约定俗成，流传下来。"

1915年，民国时期著名报人曹聚仁来杭州，那时他15岁。50年后，他回忆起当时游历过的断桥："那时的断桥，还是如乡村常见的石桥，一级一级叠着的。后来公路铺成了，石桥也就不见了。"现存的断桥是1921年重建的，改石级为平坡，加设60厘米厚的水泥混凝土拱券。

除了"段家桥"的说法，断桥还被叫作"短桥"，有词写道："荡漾香魂何处？长桥月，短桥月。"短桥，与长桥呼应。

许仙和白娘子的爱情传说是断桥上著名的浪漫故事。随着"西湖美景三月天"的歌声，断桥也成了情侣们的热门打卡地。

走过断桥，沿白堤往西，是锦带桥。虽然知名度不如断桥，但锦带桥也是白堤上一处极佳的观景点，桥上视野开阔，近可观平湖秋月，远可望孤山。

风物滋养文化，文化成为风景，西湖春天的故事，从白堤开始。

俯瞰西湖雪景，白堤
Snowy Baidi Causeway

西湖白堤，桃红柳绿
Springtime at West Lake: Red Peach Trees and Green Willows Lining Baidi Causeway

Bai Juyi's Query: Who Built Baidi Causeway?

Baidi Causeway

West Lake

Every March is the peak season for Baidi Causeway around West Lake. The peach blossoms resemble a veil of red mist, and the green willows look like a haze of smoke, creating the impression for many people that this is the quintessential springtime scene at West Lake.

You may walk along Baidi Causeway many times, but you don't always really know it.

In early 2024, the editorial board of *Yaowen Jiaozi* ("being overfastidious in wording") released the top ten Chinese wording mistakes of 2023. The seventh mistake was attributing the construction of "Baidi Causeway" to Bai Juyi.

The most famous embankments around West Lake are Baidi Causeway, Sudi Causeway, and Yanggong Causeway. It is well-known that Sudi Causeway was built by Su Dongpo and Yanggong Causeway by Yang Mengying. However, the builder of Baidi Causeway remains a mystery. It is certain that Bai Juyi had nothing to do with the construction of Baidi Causeway.

As Bai Juyi wrote in his poem, "The causeway paved with white sand is shaded by green willows", the "White Sand Causeway" is Baidi Causeway. Bai Juyi himself was also curious about who built this causeway.

Baidi Causeway is like a ribbon in West Lake. In spring, willows sprout green buds and peach blossoms smile, making it the best Instagrammable time of year to visit.

The best way to explore Baidi Causeway is by walking. The 987-meter-long, 33-meter-wide embankment runs across West Lake, naturally dividing it into inner and outer lakes. Willows and peach trees line both sides of this embankment. The view of "peach trees among willows" has become Baidi Causeway's most renowned springtime attraction.

In spring, the causeway is lined with red peach trees and green willows. In summer, lotus flowers bloom in the inner lake, echoing the ancient poem: "Boundless lotus leaves link up to the sky; lotus flowers are ultra red under sunshine." In autumn, Baidi Causeway offers the best vantage point to admire the green and yellow sycamores along Beishan Street. In winter, the "Lingering Snow on Broken Bridge" scene adds to West Lake's poetic charm.

Besides peach trees and willows, even the evergreen grass on Baidi Causeway is often newsworthy for its beauty.

To maintain the greenery, the grass in the green belt of Baidi Causeway is re-seeded again every autumn and winter, a process technically termed lawn re-greening, also known as re-seeding. In spring and summer, the grass along the causeway is Chinese lawngrass, a heat-resistant but not cold-resistant warm-season grass. In late autumn, as cold days arrive, it begins to wither, affecting the causeway's beauty. At this time, it is time to re-seed the lawn with a type of cold-resistant, cold-season grass called ryegrass.

Ryegrass can grow normally in winter, and in spring, the underground Chinese lawngrass seeds begin to germinate again, eventually taking over from the ryegrass. Chinese lawngrass and ryegrass take turns, ensuring an evergreen lawn along Baidi Causeway all year round. This isn't just about growing grass; it's about nurturing the romance and warmth of West Lake.

Many people believe that Baidi Causeway was built by Bai Juyi. In fact, there was indeed a "Baigong Causeway" in the history of West Lake, but it is not the same as the current Baidi Causeway.

In 822 CE, Bai Juyi became the governor of Hangzhou at the age of 50. Bai Juyi always felt a deep connection with Hangzhou. As a young man, he spent some time living with his father there, so he never forgot the poetic lakescape of this prestigious city south of the Yangtze River.

Although Bai Juyi served as the governor of Hangzhou for less than two years, he was a pivotal figure in the development history of West Lake and Hangzhou. During his time in Hangzhou, Bai Juyi wrote famous poems such as "On Qiantang Lake in Spring" and "Spring Sights in Hangzhou". Additionally, he was a down-to-earth and "exemplary official", serving the people by mobilizing locals to build the embankment along West Lake and dredge six wells.

It is worth mentioning that during his term of office, Bai Juyi initiated a massive project—the construction of a dike between the upper lake (now known as West Lake) and the lower lake. After the dike was completed, the upper lake was able to store more water, ensuring that Hangzhou's thousands of hectares of fertile fields had sufficient irrigation and that the city's residents had enough drinking water.

Bai Juyi did not want to raise taxes to fund the construction of the dike. To avoid increasing the burden on the people, he mobilized local resources by recruiting workers in exchange for food. Additionally, he donated part of his salary and visited temples in Hangzhou to raise funds.

In 823 CE, the construction finally started. Two months before his departure, in March of the fourth year of Emperor Muzong's Changqing reign (824 CE) of the Tang Dynasty, the dike was finally completed. He wrote "The Stone Record of Qiantang Lake" and had it carved on a stone by the lake, sharing his experience and story of regulating West Lake for future generations.

The dike built by Bai Juyi wound through the northeast of West Lake, stretching from Shihan Bridge outside the old Qiantang Gate to the old Wulin Gate. It was known as "Baigong Causeway", which is slightly different in name from "Baidi Causeway". Records of the Baigong Causeway can be found in both *The Biography of Bai Juyi* in *New History of the Tang Dynasty* and *West Lake Tour Records*.

"I can't leave Hangzhou; half my reason for staying is this lake." Bai Juyi spent less time in Hangzhou than Su Dongpo, another "mayor" of the city, but made monumental achievements during his term of service. Bai Juyi expressed his deep affection for Hangzhou in his poetry. Years later, his poem "Reminiscing Jiangnan" inspired a longing for Hangzhou in many people: "Jiangnan is beautiful. I knew its waterscape well some time ago. At daybreak, the red flowers by the river rival fire. The springtime river is greener than the green dye. How can I not remember the lovely Jiangnan?"

Over the course of history, Hangzhou's geography has changed significantly, and there's no longer any trace of "Baigong Causeway".

Who built today's Baidi Causeway? This question was also asked by Bai Juyi.

Outside of his daily work, Bai Juyi loved to stroll along "the causeway paved with white sand and shaded by green willows", which is now known as Baidi Causeway. While becoming intoxicated by the pleasing sights along Baidi Causeway, the knowledgeable poet asked himself, "Who opens a southwest lane to the temple scene?"

In other words, Baidi Causeway existed long before Bai Juyi arrived in Hangzhou.

Historically, many have investigated the mystery of "the builder of Baidi Causeway", but none have provided a definitive and justified answer. According to ancient records, in the second year of Emperor Yizong's Xiantong reign (861 CE), Cui Yan, Governor of Hangzhou constructed Baidi Causeway while building a sand embankment to prevent the Qianjiang River's tide from flooding Hangzhou. However, he arrived in Hangzhou more than 30 years after Bai Juyi, so Baidi Causeway could not have been built by him.

Que Weimin, an expert in Hangzhou's water conservancy history, uncovered the true origin of Baidi Causeway in his paper "Baidi Causeway in Qiantang Lake and Baidi Causeway in West Lake" through documentary evidence and scientific investigation.

Before West Lake was formed, the water flowed around the northern and southern sides of Gushan Hill. Due to friction and other factors, the flow rate gradually slowed down. As the water flow rejoined at the eastern end of Gushan Hill, sediment began to accumulate. This deposition gradually pushed the confluence forward. Over time, a sand dike naturally formed along the confluence of the currents. The artificial filling of Baidi Causeway began after West Lake was cut off from the Qiantang River and became a freshwater lake, roughly during the Dali reign of Emperor Daizong (766−779 CE) of the Tang Dynasty.

The formation of today's Baidi Causeway can be divided into two periods. The first period, from 2500 years ago to the beginning of the Tang Dynasty, saw Baidi Causeway in Qiantang Lake as a natural formation. The second period, starting in the mid-Tang Dynasty, involved the creation of an artificial causeway in West Lake using dredged mud. Both causeways are successive in time and interconnected in their layers of accumulation.

Historically, Baidi Causeway collapsed during the Yuan Dynasty and was not rebuilt until 1589, the seventeenth year of the Wanli reign of Emperor Shenzong during the Ming Dynasty, along with Jindai Bridge and Chuilu Pavilion. In 1724, the second year of Emperor Yongzheng's reign during the Qing Dynasty, Baidi Causeway was raised and widened to dredge West Lake. It was re-lined with flowers, peach trees, and willows.

Probably from the Qing Dynasty onwards, people gradually began to call "White Sand Causeway" by the name Baidi Causeway to commemorate Bai Juyi's contributions to Hangzhou and West Lake. Since then, Baidi Causeway, with its unique beauty, has gained additional cultural significance. Although it is incorrect to credit Bai

Juyi as the builder of Baidi Causeway, this misconception has been so deeply ingrained in people's minds for thousands of years that it is difficult to correct. As tourists stroll along Baidi Causeway, taking in the enchanting green willows and misty hills, they can't help but remember the great mayor and poet.

Besides the stunning natural lakescape, Baidi Causeway also boasts numerous cultural landmarks. Following Bai Juyi, countless scholars and poets have left their mark on Baidi Causeway, where "the vibrant flowers gradually dazzle the eyes and the lush grass can barely cover the horses' hooves." Wanghu Pavilion, where Su Dongpo once watched the rain, is located next to Baidi Causeway. The "trace of the long causeway" mentioned by Ming Dynasty prose writer and historian Zhang Dai in his essay "Viewing the Snow Scene from the Mid-Lake Pavilion" refers to Baidi Causeway.

Another notable attraction on Baidi Causeway is Duanqiao Bridge ("Broken Bridge"). Duanqiao Bridge at one end of Baidi Causeway serves as the gateway to West Lake. Stepping onto it feels like approaching West Lake, making Duanqiao Bridge a symbol of the lake. "Lingering Snow on Broken Bridge", one of the Ten Sights of West Lake, is difficult to witness because Hangzhou's winters are cold but rarely snowy.

Here's a trivia: Duanqiao Bridge was originally named after the Duan family. To this day, the outer side of the railings above Duanqiao Bridge's arch stone still bears the inscription "Duanjiaqiao" ("Bridge of the Duan Family").

Zhong Xiangping, vice president of the Hangzhou Historical Society, explained the origin of Duanjiaqiao: "In ancient times, transportation was inconvenient, so landmarks like mountains, rivers, or bridges were often named arbitrarily. This bridge over West Lake might have been named 'Duanjiaqiao' because many local residents were from the Duan family, or perhaps the Duan family contributed to its construction. The name became widely recognized and has been passed down as part of local customs and traditions. "

In 1915, at the age of 15, Cao Juren, a renowned newsman from the Republic of China, visited Hangzhou. Fifty years later, he recalled his memory of Duanqiao Bridge: "Back then, it was an ordinary stone bridge with stairs, like those in the countryside. Later, when the stone bridge was paved with a highway, the stairs disappeared." The current Duanqiao Bridge was rebuilt in 1921, replacing the stairs with a flat slope and adding a 60-centimeter thick cement concrete arch.

In addition to the legendary name "Duanjiaqiao", the bridge was once called Duanqiao ("短桥" , literally meaning "Short Bridge"), as mentioned in a poem: "Where are fragrant souls wandering? The clear moon mirrored under the long bridge, and the clear moon under the short bridge." The short bridge complements the long bridge.

The tale of Xu Xian and Lady White Snake is a famous romantic story set on Duanqiao Bridge. With the popular line "Charming West Lake in March" from the theme song of a TV drama adapted from this tale, Duanqiao Bridge has become an Instagram-worthy spot for couples.

Walk across Duanqiao Bridge and along Baidi Causeway westbound, and you will meet Jindai Bridge. Although not as famous as Duanqiao Bridge, Jindai Bridge offers the best sightseeing spot on Baidi Causeway. Here, you can enjoy a close look at the "Autumn Moon over Calm Lake" scene and also view Gushan Hill in the distance.

The scenery nourishes the culture, and the culture enhances the scenery. The story of West Lake's springtime begins at Baidi Causeway.

俯瞰西湖白堤
An Aerial View of Baidi
Causeway in West Lake

夏日西湖，晚霞很美，断桥被夕阳余晖照亮
Duanqiao Bridge over West Lake Bathed in the Spectacular
Sunset Glow on a Summer Day

世外桃源赵公堤

赵公堤 ●

西湖

　　春天的西湖，让人怦然心动。除了姹紫嫣红的百花香，还有深浅浓淡的草木绿。

　　如果你想要认真感受一番西湖的绿意盎然，向你推荐一处隐于山水间的小众秘境——赵公堤。

　　西湖的堤，个个都出名。前有苏堤和白堤，一纵一横，几乎代言了西湖四季的美；后有杨公堤，由明代杭州知府杨孟瑛主持修建，因堤上六座拱桥起起伏伏，车辆过桥时会营造出失重感，成了杭州人心中著名的"西湖过山车"路线。

　　唯有赵公堤，其知名度远不如其他三堤，游客也很少踏足，甚至许多老杭州都不一定知道它的具体位置。

　　这条深藏不露的低调小堤，已经在西湖边静静躺了近800年。

　　赵公堤紧依着杭州花圃，一头连着杨公堤，另一头连着灵隐路，仅仅几步之遥，一旦步入其中，就仿佛隔绝了车水马龙的城市喧嚣。夹岸花柳，曲径通幽，很适合在莺燕呢喃的春日漫步。

　　赵公堤的历史比杨公堤更早，早在南宋时期就修筑起来了，后几经废弃，又几经整修，才有了现在的模样。

赵公堤是谁修的？

这位"赵公"来头可不小，相传是南宋末年的临安（今杭州）知府赵与筹，一位低调的"杭州老市长"。

但他的家世背景一点也不低调：他是宋朝宗室，宋太祖赵匡胤十世孙，嘉定十三年（1220）中进士，官至吏部尚书；曾三任苏州知府，还担任过扬州、镇江等地知府，其中政绩最为突出的就是在杭州。

虽说"赵市长"的名号不如"白市长""苏市长"响亮，但他胜在"待机"时间超长。在南宋定都临安的 138 年里，知府这个位子前后有 140 多人坐过，差不多不到一年就要换人，而赵与筹一干就是 11 年，成为整个南宋时期任职时间最长的"市长"，且颇有政绩，深受百姓爱戴。

赵与筹来杭州当知府这一年已经 61 岁，本该是享清福的年纪，但他踌躇满志，有远大的政治理想和抱负。

跟历任杭州市"市长"一样，"疏浚西湖"是一项绕不开的重点工作。

淳祐七年（1247），西湖大旱水涸，百姓用水困难，朝廷诏令他迅速开湖疏浚，解决燃眉之急，要求"四至并依古岸，不许存留菱荷"。

赵与筹立即派人清理湖面上杂乱的菱和茭，又深挖湖底，挖出了很多淤泥。用淤泥在苏堤边堆了一条支堤出来。

赵与筹修筑的这条小堤，长二百五十丈（约合今 830 米）、宽二十五尺（约合今 8.3 米）。

他提前规划好，将堤的两端连接至苏堤东浦桥与洪春桥曲院风荷一带，这样，去灵隐寺的杭州百姓就可以走这条平路，不用再翻山越岭，极大地方便了香客。

虽然堤不长，但不缺景。赵与筹以苏堤为活样板，命人在这条小堤上一路插柳种花，修建亭台楼阁，重现小桥流水人家，使这里一年四季景色宜人。

关于这条堤的名字，最早叫"小新堤"。南宋周密《武林旧事》中提到："小新堤，以通灵竺之路，中作四面堂三亭，夹岸花柳，比苏堤，或名'赵公堤'。"因在南宋时，苏堤被称为"新堤"，时人为了区分，就把赵与筹修筑的新堤称为"小新堤"；后人为了纪念他，又改称其为"赵公堤"，沿用至今。

明清时，赵公堤湮废。到民国期间此地修建马路后，更是已经断续难辨。

今天我们看到的赵公堤，是 2003 年修复杨公堤至灵隐路段时重修的，仅仅是古赵公堤的一小段。沿途亭台楼阁也都是现代建筑，但依稀可以看出当年"赵市长"规划修筑时的模样。

除了赵公堤之外，"赵市长"还在杭州做了大量的城市基建工作，是一位实干型干部。

据《这里是杭州·人物》书中记录，在赵与筹担任杭州知府 11 年间，他几次疏浚西湖，重修各种堤坝，治理西湖六井，从天目山引水入城，很好地解决了杭州居民的饮水问题；他还重修了涌金门外当时非常有名的娱乐场所丰乐楼，并在涌金门北造了一个玉莲堂。他又重修了湖心亭里的放生池，在玉泉造了两个养着"异鱼"的池子。

不只这些，赵与筹还关爱百姓，在临安设置慈幼局，支给钱米，收养遗弃儿童，雇请贫妇乳养。他在任期内还为杭州新建了四个大粮仓，以保证整个城市有足够的粮食储备，又增建了新的消防设施，创建了南宋期间最专业的救火队伍，还创建了施药局，为百姓免费看病。

赵与筹卸任杭州知府时已经 71 岁，在人均寿命不长的古代，这已经算是长寿了。退休后的他，是否也曾到过自己修筑的赵公堤上踏青春游？

在春季，沿着赵公堤漫步，一路上都是幽幽小径，溪水潺潺，满眼绿意。快靠近杨公堤这头时，会看到一座别致的小桥——毓秀桥。

这座桥并不是西湖景观中以前就有的古桥，它原在萧山区新塘街道涝湖村，清道光九年（1829），里人陈有尚出资修建。毓秀桥为单孔石拱桥，造型优美，东侧桥楣石镌刻"毓秀"二字，桥心石刻八卦图案。2003 年，按原貌迁移保护至赵公堤。春天，桥边艳丽夺目的红花檵木开得正盛，古桥、红花相映成趣，拍照的话非常"出片"。

沿着长堤，还可以参观始建于宋代的小隐园。这里面积不大，属于花圃的园中园。三座仿古别墅，分别由曲折廊桥连接，小桥流水，楼阁水榭，是典型的江南私家园林。

除了风景，赵公堤上还有人文景观。著名京剧表演艺术家盖叫天的故居也在赵公堤上，叫燕南寄庐。这是一座白墙青瓦的江南民居，满墙的爬山虎层层叠叠，匍匐蔓延。盖叫天一生大多数时间都生活于此。盖叫天原名张英杰，号燕南，河北高阳县人。他十分讲究造型美，"立如松，坐如钟，卧如弓，行如风"是他恪守的人物造型准则。他开创了京剧表演中独具一格的艺术风格，世称"盖派"，最经典的形象是他塑造的武松。

　　盖叫天十分喜欢这座江南庭院，院子里树茂花繁，环境清静，是一处修身养性、练功习艺的佳地。他在这里接待过梅兰芳、周信芳等著名同行艺人。周恩来、陈毅等老一辈革命家也曾来此拜访。

盖叫天故居
Gai Jiaotian's Former Residence

赵公堤
Zhaogong Causeway

毓秀桥畔，红花檵木盛开
Loropetalum Chinense Var. Rubrum in Full Bloom Beside Yuxiu Bridge

水中的木桩
Wooden Stakes in Water

春色迷人
Captivating Spring Scenery

流水潺潺
A Bubbling Brook Waterfall

Zhaogong Causeway: Never-Never Land

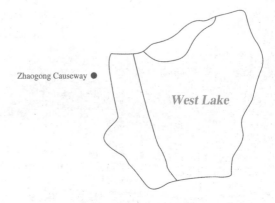

Zhaogong Causeway ●

West Lake

The springtime at West Lake is eye-catching and heart-delighting. Alongside the lingering aromas of diverse flowers, there are shades of green grass and trees.

To truly experience the greenness of West Lake, we recommend the hidden gem nestled among the hills and rivers: Zhaogong Causeway.

The causeways of West Lake are all renowned, each offering a unique blend of natural beauty and historical significance. Sudi Causeway and Baidi Causeway divide West Lake vertically and horizontally, enhancing its beauty throughout all seasons. Yanggong Causeway, constructed under the leadership of Yang Mengying, the Governor of Hangzhou Prefecture during the Ming Dynasty, features six arch bridges. These bridges give passengers a sense of weightlessness when crossing, earning the route the nickname "West Lake Roller Coaster Route" among locals.

Zhaogong Causeway is far less popular than the other three causeways. It is the least-visited by tourists, and even many longtime residents of Hangzhou may not know its exact location.

This small, unassuming embankment has quietly stood by West Lake for nearly 8 centuries.

Zhaogong Causeway is near the Hangzhou Flower Garden, with one end connected to Yanggong Causeway and the other to Lingyin Road. Just a few steps in, and you'll feel as if you've been transported away from the hustle and bustle of the city.

With flowers and willows lining the causeway, it's the perfect place for a leisurely stroll along the winding path during this season of chirping birds and warbling swallows.

The history of Zhaogong Causeway dates back even earlier than Yanggong Causeway. It was originally built during the Southern Song Dynasty and has undergone several periods of abandonment and refurbishment to achieve its current appearance.

Who was its builder?

"Zhaogong" is said to refer to Zhao Yuchou, the governor of Lin'an (present-day Hangzhou) during the late Southern Song Dynasty. He was a modest and unassuming figure, often referred to as the "old mayor of Hangzhou".

Despite his modest demeanor, Zhao Yuchou came from a prestigious background, being a descendant of the Song Dynasty's imperial clan and the tenth grandson of Emperor Taizu. He passed the imperial examination in the 13th year of Emperor Ningzong's Jiading reign(1220) and held several important positions, including Minister of the Ministry of Official Personnel Affairs. He also served as Governor of Suzhou Prefecture three times, as well as Governor of Yangzhou, Zhenjiang, and / as well as other prefectures. His most notable political achievements were all made in Hangzhou.

Although "Mayor Zhao" is not as famous as "Mayor Bai" and "Mayor Su", he was well-known for his longest tenure. The Southern Song Dynasty made Lin'an the capital for 138 years. During this period, over 140 officials alternated in the post of Hangzhou Governor, with the average term lasting less than a year. However, once Zhao Yuchou assumed office, he served for 11 years, becoming the longest-serving "mayor". He made remarkable achievements in governing the city and was highly esteemed and loved by the public.

In fact, when Zhao Yuchou became Governor of Hangzhou, he was already 61 years old. He should have retired to enjoy a leisurely life, but he was still full of ambition and had strong political ideals and aspirations.

Like all the governors before him from previous dynasties, dredging West Lake was at the top of his agenda.

In the seventh year of Emperor Lizong's Chunyou reign (1247), a severe drought dried up West Lake, making it extremely difficult to ensure the local water supply. The imperial court ordered Zhao Yuchou to take advantage of the drought to dredge West Lake and address the pressing water management issue. The directive required that "the lake be dredged along its four sides down to its original banks, without leaving any lotus or water chestnut plants".

He immediately mobilized people to remove the tangled lotus and water chestnut plants from the lake's surface and dredge the bottom, extracting a large amount of silt. He built an offshoot dike with the extracted silt alongside Sudi Causeway.

This small dike measures 250 *zhang* in length (approximately over 830 meters) and 25 *chi* in width (about 8.3 meters).

According to his plan, this dike connects Dongpu Bridge on Sudi Causeway to Hongchun Bridge near the "Lotus in the Breeze at Crooked Courtyard" scene. This allows Hangzhou locals and Buddhist pilgrims to reach Lingyin Temple via this flat road without having to hike up the mountains, greatly facilitating their trips.

Short as this dike is, it boasts an abundance of sights. Modeling this dike after Sudi Causeway, Zhao Yuchou had willows and flowers planted, and pavilions, small bridges, and waterfalls constructed all along the causeway, ensuring the scenery is pleasing in all seasons.

Initially, this causeway was named Xiaoxin Causeway. According to *Memories of Hangzhou* written by Zhou Mi during the Southern Song Dynasty: "Xiaoxin Causeway leads to a road to Lingyin Temple, lined with willows and flowers. In the middle, there is a hall with windows open in all four directions and three pavilions. The causeway is adjacent to Sudi Causeway, also known as 'Zhaogong Causeway'." During the Southern Song Dynasty, Sudi Causeway was known as "Xin Causeway". To distinguish it from the new causeway built by Zhao Yuchou, the locals at that time referred to Zhaogong Causeway as "Xiaoxin Causeway" (meaning "the little new causeway"). In honor of Zhao Yuchou, they renamed it Zhaogong Causeway, a name that is still in use today.

During the Ming and Qing Dynasties, Zhaogong Causeway was abandoned. When highways were constructed in this area during the Republic of China, the causeway became ruined in many parts and difficult to recognize.

Today's Zhaogong Causeway was rebuilt in 2003 during the restoration of the section from Yanggong Causeway to Lingyin Road, which is only a small part of the original causeway. The pavilions along the way are modern structures, but you can still get a vague sense of what it looked like when Mayor Zhao initially planned and built it.

In addition to Zhaogong Causeway, Mayor Zhao also undertook numerous urban infrastructure projects in Hangzhou, demonstrating his dedication as a practical and committed official.

According to *Here is Hangzhou: Celebrities*, during his 11 years as governor of Hangzhou, Zhao Yuchou dredged West Lake multiple times to rebuild various dikes and dams. He also dredged six wells connected to West Lake. Additionally, he led efforts to transfer water from Tianmu Mountain into the city, effectively solving Hangzhou's drinking water shortage. He rebuilt Fengle Mansion, a renowned entertainment venue outside Yongjin Gate, and constructed Yulian Hall to the north of Yongjin Gate. He restored the life-release pool in Huxin Pavilion and constructed two pools for "precious fish" near Yuquan Spring.

Zhao Yuchou showed great care for the people by establishing orphanages in Lin'an. He provided funds and food to support abandoned children and hired impoverished women to breastfeed the babies. During his tenure, he also constructed four new granaries in Hangzhou to ensure the city had sufficient food reserves. Interestingly, he established new firefighting facilities and created the most professional firefighting team of the Southern Song Dynasty. Additionally, he established the Medicine Bureau to offer free medical treatment to the people.

When Zhao Yuchou stepped down as mayor of Hangzhou at the age of 71, he was considered a long-lived old man, especially given the shorter life expectancy in ancient times. It is unknown whether he, after his retirement, ever visited Zhaogong Causeway, which he had personally built, during the springtime.

In spring, a stroll along Zhaogong Causeway will reveal secluded paths, gurgling streams, and lush greenery all around. As you approach Yanggong Causeway, you'll come across a chic bridge called Yuxiu Bridge.

Originally, this bridge is not an ancient bridge as part of West Lake's lakescape but an old bridge located in Laohu Village of Xintang Sub-district, Xiaoshan District. Its construction was funded by a local philanthropist, Chen Youshang, in the nineth year of Emperor Daoguang's reign (1829). The bridge is a gracefully shaped, single-span stone arch bridge. The keystone on its eastern side was engraved with the characters "Yuxiu" (literally meaning "richly endowed with natural resources that nurture excellent talents"), and the stone in the middle of its roadway was engraved with the Eight Trigrams. In 2003, this bridge was relocated to Zhaogong Causeway, preserving its original appearance, for the sake of protection. In spring, the Loropetalum chinense var. rubrum next to Yuxiu Bridge is in full bloom. The ancient bridge and the vibrant red flowers complement each other beautifully. If you take photos of them, you are sure to capture some stunning shots.

If you continue walking along this dike, you can also visit Xiaoyin Garden, which was built during the Song Dynasty. It is a miniature garden within a garden. It features three antiqued villas connected by zigzag corridor bridges, surrounded by flowing water and pavilions. This is a typical example of a private garden in Jiangnan.

In addition to its natural scenery, Zhaogong Causeway is also home to various cultural landmarks. The former residence of the renowned Peking Opera performer Gai

Jiaotian, known as "Yannan Jilu" ("the villa of Yannan"), is also located on Zhaogong Causeway. This is a typical Jiangnan residential building, with black tiles and white walls covered with clusters of creeping and spreading creepers. Gai Jiaotian spent most of his life living here. He was originally called Zhang Yingjie, with the literary name Yanan, and was born in Gaoyang County, Hebei Province. When performing Peking Opera, he focused on the beauty of his role, adhering to the principle: "Stand like a pine, sit like a table clock, rest like a bow, walk like the wind." His unique artistic style, known as the "Gai School", is best exemplified by his performance as Wu Song, a tiger-slaying hero.

He loved this Jiangnan-style courtyard for its quiet and peaceful atmosphere, lush trees, and variety of flowers. It was the perfect place for him to cultivate his body and mind and practice his opera performing skills. He hosted revolutionaries such as Zhou Enlai and Chen Yi here, as well as renowned fellow artists like Mei Lanfang and Zhou Xinfang.

燕南寄廬

盖叫天故居
Gai Jiaotian's Former Residence

金沙港
Jinsha Port

白塔下杏花盛开
Apricot Flowers in Full Bloom near
the White Pagoda

千年白塔，
百年铁路

● 白塔公园

　　说到钱塘江畔的古塔，大家首先想到的应该是六和塔，它伫立在月轮山上，是杭州一处地标性建筑。

　　就在六和塔不远处，位于之江路与老复兴路之间的白塔公园里，还有另一座千年古塔，却常年低调。作为公园主角的白塔，始建于五代十国时期的吴越国末期，如今已经1000多岁了。

　　吴越国的历代国王都虔诚信佛，虽然在杭州统治不到百年，但大兴佛事建筑，使杭州逐渐成为全国的佛教中心，寺院遍布、佛塔林立，有了"东南佛国"的响亮名号。与白塔同时期一兴而起的，还包括净慈寺、慈云岭龛像、南高峰山腰的烟霞寺等。

　　在众多杭州佛教建筑中，白塔堪称精品之一，它代表着五代吴越国时期最顶级的工艺水平和最经典的建筑风格。

　　白塔共九层，高14.4米，由61块白色太湖石拼接砌筑而成，是仿木结构楼阁式的八边九级石塔。每层都由塔身、塔檐和平座三部分组成，塔身上雕刻的佛教图像精美细致，现存133尊造像。1988年，它被国务院公布为全国重点文物保护单位。

白塔与灵隐寺内的双石塔还有"亲缘"关系。20世纪30年代，梁思成应邀来杭州商讨六和塔重修计划，妻子林徽因和助手刘致平陪他同行。工作之余，他们一起来到六和塔旁边的闸口，专门对白塔做了测绘和研考。跟当时的六和塔一样，两座历经损毁的千年古塔，彼时都已伤痕累累。

他们惊讶地发现，"闸口白塔除去极少部分外，作风规制几乎与灵隐双塔完全相同……"梁思成认为，灵隐寺大雄宝殿前东西两侧的双石塔，与白塔不仅是同一时期的，甚至有很大可能是出自同一工匠之手。

梁思成将这个重要发现写成了《闸口白塔及灵隐寺双石塔》一文，原定准备发表于民国26年（1937）《中国营造学社汇刊》的《塔》专刊中，这也是对白塔最早的研究。

然而，因抗日战争全面爆发，这些关于闸口白塔的图纸和文稿只得沉积箱底，没能发表，直到40年后，1986年9月才收录在《梁思成文集》中出版，那一年，梁思成与林徽因早已不在人世。

历经千年风雨，白塔犹如一位饱经沧桑的老人，记录下岁月留下的斑驳痕迹。塔下的闸口白塔陈列馆值得走进去看看，里面详细记录了白塔的前世今生。

吴越王当年选定在这里修建白塔，是有讲究的，因其与"龙"有关。

白塔公园内有一条龙山河。龙山，指的是玉皇山，白塔公园地处玉皇山南，龙山河就在龙山脚下。

龙山河实际上就是中河的南段。中河连通京杭大运河和钱塘江，以凤山水城门为界，北面称中河，南面称为龙山河。因钱塘江水位比龙山河高，为防止江水倒灌入城，五代十国时期，吴越国国王钱镠在河的入江口设了"两闸"，靠江的称"浙江闸"，靠山的称"龙山闸"。这里也是古京杭大运河的南端起点，杭州人把这一带叫作"闸口"。

吴越时期，南北航运发达，为了指引船舶安全航行，同时也起到祭祀江神的作用，钱镠的孙子钱弘佐就在龙山东面的白塔岭上建起了一座白塔。江商海商的四方百货，从白塔渡口进杭州城内，都需翻坝"闸口"，这也是钱塘江进入京杭大运河的唯一通道。据说当时，在现在六和塔至美政桥一带的江涂上，货物等着进入龙山河，经常形成长达数公里的停靠区，昔日这里的繁忙与人气可想而知。

古闸如今已经不在，只留下遗址，但千年龙山河依然静静流淌，跟白塔一起，阅尽繁华无数，见证历史变迁。

白塔陈列馆外是一个大型广场，叫南宋地经广场。南宋时，白塔邻近皇城，闸口这里就成了进入皇城的必经之地，传说当时有人在这里卖"地经"——《朝京里程图》，相当于现在的旅游交通图，上面标注着临安城的所属来往通道、里程和驿站等。有一首诗"白塔桥边卖地经，长亭短驿甚分明。如何只说临安路，不数中原有几程？"用来讥讽偏安一隅的南宋朝廷。

现在的广场是 2014 年白塔公园开园时打造的，共设 8 块石质大地图，与南宋时期的上八府对应，它们的轮廓和位置关系也都参照了南宋浙江版图，镌刻了南宋时期山、城、水、路的关系。

除了白塔和龙山河，公园里还有另外一道风景——铁路和火车。

园内保留着两段平行的废旧铁轨，这是著名的江墅铁路杭州段的起点，它是浙江省历史上第一条铁路，因从钱塘江畔逶迤至拱墅而得名。

清光绪三十三年（1907），江墅铁路全线通车并开始客货运营，沿途从南至北设闸口、南星、清泰（今天的城站火车站）、艮山和拱宸 5 个站。

清宣统元年（1909），沪杭甬铁路沪杭段通车运营，江墅铁路闸口至艮山门段成了沪杭铁路的一部分，而沪杭铁路正是今天沪杭高铁的前身。

民国元年（1912）12 月 11 日，时任全国铁路督办的孙中山来到闸口考察江墅铁路和钱塘江水道。他饶有兴致地坐上火车一路到了拱宸桥，体验了一把这条长度仅有 16 公里的铁路。

民国 18 年（1929），浙江省建成浙赣铁路。乘坐沪杭线的旅客，须从闸口站下车，坐船渡过波涛汹涌的钱塘江，再登上浙赣线的火车继续旅行；从浙赣线坐火车过来的旅客，也在闸口站换乘往嘉兴、上海方向的火车。闸口火车站成为沪杭、浙赣两大干线的中转站。鼎盛时期，火车站附近的甘水巷聚集 8 家饭馆，还有茶馆、酒馆和多家旅馆。

之后，闸口站又见证了钱塘江大桥的建成通车，也见证了一批又一批杭州知青北上。

时光流转，闸口车站经历了各种身份转换：从客运站、货运站到机务段，后来成了南星桥客运站的货场，两排场房之间还保留了当时货运的铁轨。

100多年过去了，曾经的车站变成了现在的公园，铁轨也成了游客可以散步的游步道。

由于整个公园的地形是狭长的，因地制宜，公园内这两条标准轨距的铁轨各有用途。一条陈列着老式火车头与车厢；另一条是能够载人的蒸汽机观光小火车，也就是网友口中那趟"开往春天的列车"。买票乘坐，可以在公园东西两头来回乘一圈，大约十分钟。在徐徐移动的车身里，时光仿佛能倒流。

除了复古的老式绿皮火车，过去的候车室也被保留了下来，自带二十世纪七八十年代特有的文艺气息。

沿铁路西行至尽头，有一座杭州铁路博物馆知青纪念馆，面积不算大，一层主要是铁路博物馆的展陈区，二层则为知青纪念馆展区。人们在这里可以了解杭州铁路事业的发展脉络，重温杭州知青的历史记忆。

除了历史古建筑与复古工业风的混搭之外，白塔公园还有另一层气质——文艺小清新，主要是满园春色赋予的。

春暖花开时节，白塔公园内繁花争艳，可以从3月中旬一直美到4月底。最先美起来的是杏花，紧接着是樱花和垂丝海棠，还有玉兰花、喷雪花、山茶花、油菜花作为配角点缀其中。

白塔公园的樱花有一大半是染井吉野樱，开起来如梦似幻，大概有220株，另外还有100余株早樱或晚樱品种。

花映古塔塔映花，春天到白塔公园走走，连空气都散发出浪漫的味道。

龙门吊
An Old Gantry Crane

蒸汽机车火车头
An Old Steam Locomotive

白塔公园，蒸汽机绿皮观光火车仿佛从远处的
六和塔下驶来，一路开往春天
The Green Steam Sightseeing Train Appears
to Head towards the Spring, Passing the Foot
of Liuhe Pagoda in the Distance

Millennium-Old White Pagoda Along with Century-Old Railroads

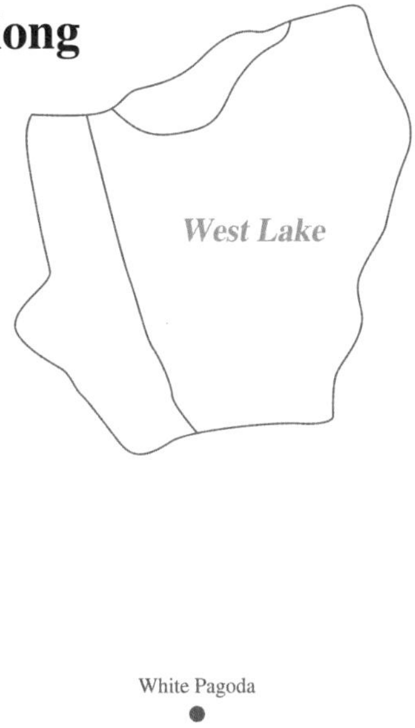

West Lake

White Pagoda

When it comes to time-honored pagodas along the Qiantang River, the first one that comes to mind is likely Liuhe Pagoda perching on top of Yuelun Hill, a notable landmark in Hangzhou.

However, near Liuhe Pagoda, within the White Pagoda Park situated between Zhijiang Road and the old Fuxing Road, there is another millennium-old but understated pagoda. The White Pagoda, the centerpiece of this park, was constructed at the end of the Wuyue State during the Five Dynasties and Ten Kingdoms period, and has stood here for over 1,000 years since then.

All the kings of the Wuyue State were devout Buddhists. Therefore, during their rule in Hangzhou, which merely lasted less than a century, they focused on constructing Buddhist architecture, including monasteries and pagodas, throughout the city. Since then, Hangzhou has become a central hub of Buddhism in China and has even earned the illustrious title of "The Buddhist Kingdom in Southeast China". The White Pagoda, Jingci Temple, the niched Buddha statues in Ciyun Ridge, and Yanxia Temple perched halfway up the Southern Peak, were all built at the same time.

Among Hangzhou's Buddhist buildings, the White Pagoda stands out with its exceptional craftsmanship and classic Wuyue architectural style from the Five Dynasties.

The White Pagoda is a nine-story, 14.4-meter-tall structure made of 61 white

Taihu stones, designed to resemble a wooden octagonal pavilion. Its each story comprises three parts: the outer body, eaves, and a gallery. The outer body is adorned with exquisite Buddhist relief sculptures, 133 of which remain intact. In 1988, it was designated a national key cultural relic protection unit by the State Council.

Interestingly, the White Pagoda is frequently associated with the Twin Stone Pagodas at Lingyin Temple. In the 1930s, Chinese architect Liang Sicheng, along with his wife Lin Huiyin and assistant Liu Zhiping, was invited to Hangzhou to discuss the reconstruction of Liuhe Pagoda. After work, they made a point of visiting Zhakou (southeast end of Fuxing Road, and east of White Pagoda Ridge) to survey and map the White Pagoda. They observed that both the White Pagoda and Liuhe Pagoda had survived a millennium but bore scars from years of destruction.

To their surprise, they found that "The White Pagoda at Zhakou closely resembles the Twin Pagodas at Lingyin Temple in architectural style..." Liang Sicheng therefore speculated that both the Twin Pagodas on the east and west sides of the main hall of Lingyin Temple and the White Pagoda were likely built not only in the same period but also by the same architect.

Later, Liang Sicheng documented his discovery in an article titled "A Study of the White Pagoda and the Twin Pagodas at Lingyin Temple", set to be published in 1937 in the *Journal of the Society for the Study of Chinese Architecture*'s special issue on pagodas. This article became the earliest study of the White Pagoda.

However, the outbreak of the war against Japanese aggression forced Liang Sicheng to hide his drawings of the White Pagoda and his article manuscript for 40 years. They were finally published in September 1986 in the *Works of Liang Sicheng*, long after both Liang Sicheng and Lin Huiyin passed away.

After a thousand years of weathering, the White Pagoda stands like an old man, marked by the traces of time. The Zhakou White Pagoda Exhibition Hall is worth a visit, offering a comprehensive view of the White Pagoda's past and present.

The King of Wuyue chose this location to build the White Pagoda because it has a connection to "long" (literally "dragon").

Within White Pagoda Park, there is a river called Longshan ("dragon hill"). "Longshan" refers to Yuhuang Hill, as the park is situated to the south of it, at the base of which flows the Longshan River.

The Longshan River is actually the southern section of the Zhonghe River, which links the Beijing-Hangzhou Grand Canal and the Qiantang River. Due to the Fengshan Watergate dividing the Zhonghe River, the northern section retains the name Zhonghe, while the southern section is known as the Longshan River. Due to the higher water level of the Qiantang River compared to the Longshan River, Wuyue King Qian Liu installed two watergates at the Longshan River's mouth to prevent flooding in Hangzhou. The watergate near the river is called "Zhejiang Gate", while the one beside the hill is named "Longshan Gate". This area marks the starting point of the southern section of the ancient Beijing-Hangzhou Grand Canal, so locals refer to it as Zhakou ("the place around a watergate").

During the Wuyue period, north-south shipping flourished. To guide ships safely and worship the river god, King Qian Hongzuo, grandson of King Qian Liu, built a white pagoda on White Pagoda Ridge, east of Longshan Hill. Water-borne or sea-borne merchandise from across China, transported via White Pagoda Ferry into Hangzhou, had to pass through the watergate—the only channel connecting the Qiantang River to the Beijing-Hangzhou Grand Canal. It's said that the shallows between present-day Liuhe Pagoda and Meizheng Bridge became a waiting area several kilometers long, where boats loaded with goods lined up to enter the Longshan River. What a bustling scene it must have been!

The old watergate is gone, leaving only ruins. However, the millennium-old Longshan River still flows quietly alongside the White Pagoda, bearing witness to countless bustling scenes and historical changes.

Outside the White Pagoda Exhibition Hall is a large square called Southern Song Map Square. During the Southern Song Dynasty, the White Pagoda was near the Imperial City of Lin'an (now Hangzhou), making Zhakou the main route to the city. Legend has it that Imperial City Maps, similar to today's tourist maps, was often sold here. These maps detailed roads, distances, and courier stations around Lin'an. There is a poem that captures the scene of the time: "By White Pagoda Bridge, city maps are sold, detailing all courier stations. How can we solely want to know the distance to Lin'an but not to the Central Plains?" This poem was used to mock the self-content isolated Southern Song court.

The current square was created when White Pagoda Park opened in 2014, featuring large stone maps of the eight provinces of Southern Zhejiang during the Southern Song Dynasty. These eight maps were modelled on the map of Zhejiang in the Southern Song Dynasty, outlining mountains, waters, and roads around the city.

Besides the White Pagoda and Longshan River, the park features two railroads and trains.

The park features two parallel sections of scrap rail tracks, marking the starting point of the Hangzhou section of the historic Jiangshu Railway, the first railroad in Zhejiang, named for its route along the Qiantang River to Gongshu.

In 1907, the Jiangshu Railway opened to traffic and began passenger and freight operations, connecting five stations from south to north: Zhakou, Nanxing, Qingtai (now Hangzhou Railway Station), Genshan, and Gongchen.

In 1909, the Shanghai-Hangzhou section of the Shanghai-Hangzhou-Ningbo Railway began operations. The section from Zhakou to Genshanmen of the Jiangshu Railway was incorporated into the Shanghai-Hangzhou Railway, the predecessor of today's Shanghai-Hangzhou High-speed Railway.

On December 11, 1912, Sun Yat-sen, who was then the governor of national railroads, visited Zhakou to inspect the Jiangshu Railway and waterways of the Qiantang River. He made a point of riding the train all the way to Gongchen Bridge, completing a brief 16-kilometer journey.

In 1929, the Zhejiang-Jiangxi Railway was completed in Zhejiang. Passengers on the Shanghai-Hangzhou line had to disembark at Zhakou Station, cross the choppy Qiantang River by boat, and then board the Zhejiang-Jiangxi line to continue their journey. Similarly, passengers from the Zhejiang-Jiangxi line switched trains at Zhakou Station to travel to Jiaxing and Shanghai. Zhakou Railway Station thus became a hub for these two main lines: Shanghai-Hangzhou and Zhejiang-Jiangxi. In Zhakou Station's heyday, nearby Ganshui Lane featured eight restaurants, along with teahouses, taverns, and hotels.

Later, the station saw the opening of the Qiantang River Bridge and a group of educated youths from Hangzhou heading north by train.

Over time, Zhakou Station served as a passenger station, freight station, and train maintenance station. It later became the freight yard for Nanxingqiao Passenger Station, with tracks for transporting goods still preserved between two rows of shed-type warehouses.

Over a century later, the former station has become a park, and its tracks have turned into a walking trail for visitors.

Due to the park's long and narrow shape, the two sections of standard-gauge rail tracks serve different purposes based on their locations. One section displays an old locomotive and carriages, while the other carries a steam engine sightseeing train, known among netizens as the "train heading to spring". A single ticket provides a ten-minute round trip between the park's east and west ends. Riding in a slow-moving carriage feels like traveling back in time.

Besides the retro green train, the waiting room has been preserved, retaining the unique artistic atmosphere of the 1970s and 1980s.

Follow the railroad west to its end, and you will find the Hangzhou Railway

Museum & Memorial Hall for Educated Youths. This small, two-floor museum features a railroad exhibition on the first floor and a Memorial Hall for Educated Youths on the second. Touring the museum will give you insight into the development of Hangzhou's railway and the history of its educated youths.

In addition to its mixed style of historical and retro industrial architecture, White Tower Park is also tinged with another quality—poetic freshness, mainly bestowed by the overflowing vigor of springtime.

In spring, all the flowers in the park bloom, competing in color and variety from mid-March until the end of April. Apricot flowers are the first to bloom in full, followed by cherry blossoms and hall crabapples. Magnolias, snowdrops, camellias, and rapeseed blossoms serve as beautiful complements.

A significant portion of the park's cherry blossoms are Somei-Yoshino sakura, known for their dreamlike flowers, totaling 220 trees, compared to over 100 Prunus pendula or Prunus lannesiana trees.

Flowers provide a backdrop that enhances the magnificence of the ancient pagoda, which in turn accentuates their vibrant colors. Take a walk in White Pagoda Park in spring, and you'll catch the romantic scent in the air.

法喜寺，500 多岁玉兰花开
An Aerial View of the Over 500-Year-Old
Yulan Magnolia, Faxi Temple

法喜寺，500 多岁玉兰花开
Over 500-Year-Old Yulan Magnolia in Bloom at Faxi Temple

如此高花白于雪，
年年偏是斗风开

西湖

法喜寺 ●

杭州上天竺法喜寺，有一株明代古玉兰，树龄已经超过 500 岁，是杭州年纪最大的玉兰树。

很多人虽然去过法喜寺多回，却一直没找到古玉兰的位置。其实，不必爬山，这株玉兰美人就端坐在客堂右手边的一处院子里。这里的匾额上写着"五观堂"，是僧人吃饭的地方。

树高超过 12 米，平均冠幅达 7.5 米，树干宽近 1 米。粗壮的树干爬满青苔，宽阔的树冠如同一把张开的巨型伞盖，在空中向四周生长，把整个庭院包覆其中。硕大又洁白的花瓣与一串串红色小灯笼交相辉映。树下是从城市四面八方慕名赶来的游人，端着相机寻找最佳拍摄角度。

杭州植物园高级工程师莫亚鹰专门研究木兰科。她说，玉兰是很长寿的树种。据史料记载，中国人种植玉兰，迄今已有 2500 多年历史，最早的玉兰都是种在寺庙和皇家庭院里的。

除了法喜寺，余杭径山寺也有两株玉兰。

径山寺始建于唐天宝年间（742—756），距今已有 1200 余年。走进径山寺，寺门口和观音殿前的两株古玉兰已是白花满树。它们的树龄分别是 315

年和 205 年，枝干粗壮，玉兰盛开时朵朵素雅白净，幽香阵阵，沁人心脾。

另外，良渚东明寺法堂前有一株古玉兰，是临济宗三十三世愚山超藏禅师在清康熙六年（1667）重修塔院时种下的。东明寺几经修缮，这棵古玉兰依旧保持挺立。

杭州灵隐寺里的玉兰花也是美得出名。玉兰树算是花树里的庞然大物，花开硕大纵情，重重叠叠，簇簇拥拥，花蕊内敛。白居易写过不少关于玉兰花的诗，其中就有和灵隐寺玉兰有关的《题灵隐寺红辛夷花，戏酬光上人》："紫粉笔含尖火焰，红胭脂染小莲花。芳情乡思知多少，恼得山僧悔出家。"白居易诗中描绘了红辛夷花之美，然后说酬光和尚也喜欢这美丽的植物，是不是后悔出家为僧了。

在初春的花里，玉兰属于"来去匆匆"的。一朵花，从花开到落败，顶多也就两三天。哪怕是一整棵树，花开花落，也不过 10 天左右。

杭州城里的玉兰品种很多。莫高工说，最早开花的叫望春玉兰，白带点红，它跟白玉兰很相似，都是 9 个花被片，但白玉兰的 9 瓣是等大的，而望春玉兰只有 6 瓣等大，还有 3 瓣是小小的。

最常见、种植数量也最多的是白玉兰，纯白色或者花朵底下带着紫色条纹；还有一种二乔玉兰，是白玉兰和紫玉兰的杂交品种，花瓣外头是紫色，里头是白色。紫玉兰，紫红色一片，开花很晚，到近 4 月初才肯"露面"。它也不像其他玉兰高高壮壮，属于落叶灌木，植株很小，矮矮的。

还有玉兰家族里的"颜值担当"——天目玉兰，这是中国特有的品种，且十分稀有。杭州植物园从 1951 年开始引种栽培天目玉兰，现园内保存有 20 余株成年植株。

此外，比较少见的品种还有飞黄玉兰和黄山玉兰等。

经常有人问：广玉兰和白玉兰怎么区分？最简单的是看花期，广玉兰通常在 5 至 6 月开花，白玉兰在 3 月。最本质的不同是，两者分类不同，广玉兰是常绿乔木，白玉兰是落叶乔木。

几乎所有玉兰都是先花后叶，盛开的时候，枝头上一片叶子也没有，一树全白都是花。只有紫玉兰是个例外，花叶同时出现。

而广玉兰因为一年四季常青，所以既不像紫玉兰那样花叶同放，也不像其他玉兰那样先开花后长叶。

玉兰的生长节律和杭州气候、季节变化很合拍。1至2月，杭州平均气温较低的时候，它在休眠；到了3月，气温回升，雨量增加，开始萌动或开花；随着气温继续升高和降水急剧增加，迅速进入旺盛生长期；9月以后，种子陆续成熟，叶片开始变色并逐渐凋落，再次进入休眠期。

玉兰还有个特别的地方，就是花苞"待机"时间超长。比如，今年3月开放的花，其实在去年6月基本就会长出花苞来，然后一直要在枝头孕育、生长大半年时间。在这个过程中，一旦气温、光照、雨水等条件适合了，有些花苞就会受刺激"异常发育"，反季节开花。

所以，你会在杭州异常温暖的秋天，看到属于春天的玉兰"错乱"开花了。

很多人喜欢玉兰，是喜欢它的冰清玉洁，外观好看。但也有些人，喜欢它的香甜——比如慈禧，传说她很爱吃油炸玉兰片，每到春季玉兰花开时，就让御膳房做了给她当休闲食品吃。

每年冬天，玉兰树上的花苞一鼓起来，植物园里的松鼠、小鸟就会去啃花苞，留空壳掉下树，可见它确实美味。

500 多岁玉兰花开
White Blossoms of the Over 500-Year-Old Yulan Magnolia

500 多岁玉兰花开
White Blossoms of the Over 500-Year-Old Yulan Magnolia

Snow-White Blooms Against Early Spring Chill

West Lake

Faxi Temple

At Faxi Temple on the upper part of Tianzhu Mountain, there is an ancient Yulan magnolia from the Ming Dynasty, now over 500 years old. It is the oldest magnolia tree in Hangzhou.

Many tourists have visited Faxi Temple multiple times but have not been able to see the ancient Yulan magnolia. In fact, tourists don't have to hike up the mountain to see it. This beauty is located in a courtyard to the right of a guest hall with an overhead plaque inscribed with "Wuguan Hall", which serves as the dining place for monks.

The Yulan magnolia tree stands over 12 meters tall, with an average crown width of 7.5 meters and a trunk nearly 1 meter in diameter. Its thick trunk is covered with moss, and its wide crown spreads out like a giant umbrella, extending in all directions and encompassing the entire courtyard. The large, white petals are adorned with strings of tiny red lanterns. Visitors from all parts of the city often stand under the tree, searching for the best angle to capture the beautiful view with their cameras.

Mo Yaying, a senior engineer at the Hangzhou Botanical Garden, specializes in magnolias. According to her, the Yulan magnolia is a very long-lived species. She noted that historical records show Yulan magnolias were initially planted in temples and royal courtyards, and it has been 2,500 years since the Chinese people first began cultivating them.

In addition to Faxi Temple, Jingshan Temple in Yuhang also has two Yulan magnolia trees that are in full bloom in Spring.

Jingshan Temple was built over 1,200 years ago during the Tianbao reign of Emperor Xuanzong in the Tang Dynasty (742−756) . Now, when tourists enter Jingshan Temple, they will find the ancient Yulan magnolia trees beside the entrance and in front of Guanyin Hall already covered with white flowers. These trees are 315 and 205 years old, respectively. When in full bloom, their thick branches and trunks are embellished with elegant, fragrant, and refreshing white flowers.

Additionally, in front of the Dharma Hall at Dongming Temple in Liangzhu, there is an ancient Yulan magnolia. This tree was planted in 1667 by the 33rd Zen Buddhism Master Chaozang of the Linji school during the temple's reconstruction. Dongming Temple has undergone several renovations, yet this ancient magnolia still thrives.

The magnolias at Lingyin Temple in Hangzhou are also renowned for their beauty. The magnolia tree is considered a giant among flowering trees, with its large, luxuriant, overlapping blooms that cluster together, and its stamens and pistils subtly hidden. Bai Juyi wrote numerous poems about the Yulan magnolia. One of these poems, titled "A Fun Question on Yulan Magnolia to Ask the Abbot of Lingyin Temple" is specifically related to the magnolias at Lingyin Temple: "Purple magnolia blooms are flames among the trees, like tiny rouge lotus flowers swaying in the breeze. How much do you miss your hometown when you see this sight? You must regret leaving home to embrace the monk's life. " In his poem, Bai Juyi described the beauty of red magnolia flowers and asked the monk, a fan of this plant, if he regretted becoming a monk.

Among early spring flowers, magnolias "bloom and wither in a hurry". The flowering period of a Yulan magnolia bloom lasts at most two or three days. An entire magnolia tree blooms and sheds its flowers within about 10 days.

Hangzhou City boasts many varieties of magnolias. Engineer Ms. Mo mentioned that the earliest blooming magnolia is Yulania biondii. Each of its flowers, white with a reddish tint, has 9 tepals similar to the white magnolia. The white magnolia has 9 petals of the same size, while Yulania biondii has 3 tiny petals and 6 larger ones of the same size.

The most common and widely planted variety is the white magnolia, with pure white flowers or white flowers with purple stripes underneath. The lily magnolia, with purple-red flowers, blooms late, nearly at the beginning of April; unlike other tall and robust magnolias, it is a small, short deciduous shrub.Another variety is Magnolia soulangeana Soul.-Bod., a hybrid of the white magnolia and lily magnolia; its petals are purple on the outside and white on the inside.

In the magnolia family, the most mesmerizing is Yulania amoena, a rare and precious species unique to China. In 1951, the Hangzhou Botanical Garden began introducing and cultivating Yulania amoena; today, there are over 20 mature trees.

The garden also houses other rare varieties, including Yulania cylindrica and Yulania denudata cv. Fei Huang.

A common question is how to distinguish between lotus magnolia and white magnolia. The easiest way is to check the flowering period: the lotus magnolia blooms in May and June, while the white magnolia blooms in March. The key difference is their classification: the lotus magnolia is an evergreen tree, while the white magnolia is deciduous.

Most magnolias bloom before their leaves appear, so when they are in full bloom, the branches are covered with white flowers and no leaves. The lily magnolia is the exception: its flowers and leaves appear simultaneously.

The lotus magnolia is evergreen year-round, so it neither blooms and grows leaves simultaneously like the lily magnolia, nor blooms before leafing out like other magnolias.

Magnolias' growth rhythm aligns well with Hangzhou's climate and seasons. In January and February, when Hangzhou's temperatures are low, magnolias are dormant. In March, with rising temperatures and increased rainfall, they start to bud or bloom. As temperatures and precipitation continue to rise, they quickly enter a period of rapid growth. After September, their seeds ripen, leaves change color and wither, and then they return to dormancy.

Additionally, magnolias are known for their exceptionally long "standby time" of budding. For example, if they bloom in March this year, their buds actually started forming in June of the previous year, developing within the branches for six months. During this budding process, if conditions like temperature, light, and rain are favorable, some buds may "grow abnormally", leading to off-season flowering.

Therefore, you'll see magnolias bloom "out of season" during unusually warm fall days in Hangzhou.

Many people love magnolias for their purity, elegance, and beauty. Some even enjoy their sweetness. For instance, legend has it that Empress Dowager Cixi loved eating fried magnolia petals. Every spring, when magnolias bloomed, she would have the imperial kitchen prepare them as a snack.

Every winter, when magnolia buds swell, squirrels and birds in the Botanical Garden nibble on them, leaving empty shells to fall from the trees. These buds must be really delicious.

500 多岁玉兰花开
Over 500-Year-Old Yulan Magnolia in Full Bloom

林间山门小道
The Paved Path through Thatched Roof Gate among Woods

花开如白鸽，
珍贵如熊猫

● 杭州植物园

坊间流传，杭州植物园里有三件镇园宝贝——天目玉兰、夏蜡梅以及珙桐。

其中的珙桐，是国家一级重点保护植物，被称为"植物界的大熊猫"。4月，正是它开花的时候。

它的花形如飞鸽展翅，整树盛放的时候，就像群鸽栖息，因此也被称为"鸽子树"。

珙桐长在灵峰笼月楼，最近的路线是从青芝坞入口进，往七星古梅的方向，沿着绿荫小径走到山腰上，可以看到小桥流水，亭台楼榭，墙面上刻着"灵峰探梅"四字。如果不是梅花盛开的季节，这里很少有人来。

越过山门小亭，是一个更加幽静的庭院，笼月楼就在这里。因地势相对较高，且周边有水系，很适合珙桐生长。

还有一个入口：从植物园南门进，慢悠悠荡到灵峰景区，过漱碧亭，到云香亭，穿过素柱黑瓦、白石围栏的瑶台，再拾级而上，就到了笼月楼。

每年4月，站在珙桐树下，抬头仰望，嫩绿的叶子不断抽出来，枝繁叶茂、"白鸽"翩翩。

植物园专家告诉我们，珙桐那两片硕大洁白的"花瓣"，实际上是叫作"总苞"的叶状结构,中间那一团紫色的"花蕊"才是真正的花。

完成授粉以后,雌花会发育成一个状似小梨的核果。果实在每年10月份成熟,核大且硬,酸涩而不堪食。珙桐的俗名"木梨子"和"水梨子"就由此而来,据说,旧时旅人会拿它聊解饥渴。

6000万年前,珙桐就已经生活在这个世界上了,它是新生代第三纪古热带植物区系的物种之一。在第四纪冰川侵袭之前,它的家族在地球上也曾繁盛一时。

第四纪冰川时期的严寒让许多地区的珙桐相继灭绝,剩下的种群只在中国南方的一些地区幸存下来。现在在湖北的神农架、贵州的梵净山、四川的峨眉山、湖南的张家界和天平山以及云南省西北部,可以看到零星或小片的天然林木。

1982年,杭州植物园结合珍稀濒危植物迁地保护工作的开展,从湖北引入了珙桐树种。珙桐的原产地海拔1200米,且生性喜阴,要在杭州生长并不容易,经过多年的精心养护,这些珙桐从2010年开始开花,一年比一年开得好。

目前,灵峰笼月楼旁比较高大的一株珙桐,和草坪对面回廊旁两株较细的珙桐,都已经开花了。杭州植物园已经成功繁育出珙桐小苗近百株,除了笼月楼,在植物分类区也能遇见开花的珙桐。

说起来,珙桐还是挺会挑地方住的,它的邻居就是100多岁的七星古梅。古梅据说是灵峰寺僧人在清朝所种,历经百年,现在仅存七丛,排列恰似北斗七星,尤以花早开迟谢著称。而现在的笼月楼所在地,正是当年的灵峰寺遗址。

灵峰,在宋代以前曾称为"鹫峰"。这里最早闻名于世的,不是梅花,当然更不是珙桐,而是寺庙。1600年前,天竺僧人慧理将佛教带来杭州,在飞来峰左右连建"灵隐""灵峰"等五寺。五代后晋开运年间(944—946),吴越王在这里建了"鹫峰禅院";北宋治平二年(1065),宋英宗又改赐额"灵峰寺"。后来,灵峰寺的香火越来越旺,成为当时杭州名刹之一,宋时以灵峰寺为北天竺,与灵隐西天竺相呼应。只不过,灵隐寺一直香火炽盛,而灵峰寺则时废时兴。

清道光年间(1821—1850),镇守杭州的副都统固庆将军,特别钟爱灵峰的幽雅,便拨资重修寺院,并在寺中立石碑《重修西湖北山灵峰寺碑记》,

如今这块石碑还矗立在灵峰探梅景区的掬月亭内。

民国年间，灵峰寺因地处偏僻，香火不盛。抗日战争杭州沦陷时，灵峰寺坍毁，僧侣星散，梅林更为凋零。至 1950 年初，仅存断墙残壁与洗钵池、掬月泉、来鹤亭。

现在看到的仿古笼月楼，是 1988 年园林部门重新修建的。

杭州植物园，珙桐花开
Blossoms of Dove Trees, Hangzhou
Botanical Garden

杭州植物园，笼月楼
Longyue Pavilion at Hangzhou Botanical Garden

杭州植物园，两棵珙桐就在"香自幽谷"回廊旁
Two Dove Trees by Winding Corridor "Xiang Zi Yougu" at Hangzhou Botanical Garden

A Plant as Rare as Giant Panda with Dove-Like Blossoms

● Hangzhou Botanical Garden

West Lake

It is said that the Hangzhou Botanical Garden has three treasures: Yulania amoena, Chinese sweetshrub, and the dove tree.

The dove tree is a first-class key plant protected at the state level, often referred to as the "giant panda of the plant world". April is the time when it blooms.

Its flowers resemble doves spreading their wings, and when the entire tree is in full bloom, it looks like a flock of doves roosting. This is why it is called "dove tree".

The dove tree grows beside Longyue Pavilion. The closest route to see it starts at the entrance of Qingzhiwu Village. Head towards the "Qixing Ancient Wintersweet" scene and follow a greenery-lined path up the hillside. Along the way, you'll come across a small bridge, a waterfall, and a few scattered pavilions. You'll also see a screen wall with the words "Plum Blossoms on Lingfeng Hill" engraved on it. If it's not plum blossom season, few tourists visit this place.

Pass through a small pavilion at the gate, and you will find yourself in an even more secluded courtyard where Longyue Pavilion is located. The high terrain and surrounding water system make this area ideal for the dove tree to grow.

Another route is to enter the Botanical Garden from its south gate and reach the Lingfeng scenic area. From there, you can pass through Shubi Pavilion, Yunxiang Pavilion, and Yaotai Pavilion with its black tiles, uncolored columns, and white stone fences, and then hike up to Longyue Pavilion.

Every April, standing under a dove tree and looking up, you will see tender green leaves sprouting, branches spreading, and lush foliage, as if you are watching "doves" flutter.

According to experts at the botanical garden, the two large white "petals" are actually called "involucres", a leaf-like structure. The purple "stamen" or "pistil" at the center of the involucres is the real flower.

After pollination, the female flower will develop into a small, pear-like drupe. The dove tree's fruit ripens in October each year. It has a large, hard core, thin flesh, and is sour and unpalatable. Due to the shape of its fruit, the dove tree is often referred to by locals as the "wooden pear" or "juicy pear". It is said that travelers in the old days would use it to quench their thirst.

Sixty million years ago, the dove tree already existed in the world as one of the species of the Cenozoic Tertiary Paleotropical flora. Its family also flourished on Earth before the onslaught of the Quaternary glaciers.

The severe cold of the Quaternary glacial period extinguished the dove tree in many areas, leaving only a few survivors in parts of southern China. Nowadays, scattered or small patches of dove trees can be found in the Shennongjia Forestry Zone in Hubei, Fanjing Mountain in Guizhou, Emei Mountain in Sichuan, Zhangjiajie and Tianping Mountain in Hunan, and northwestern Yunnan Province.

In 1982, the Hangzhou Botanical Garden introduced the dove tree from Hubei as part of a conservation effort for rare and endangered plants. The dove tree originates from an altitude of 1200 meters and is a shade-loving species that doesn't easily thrive in Hangzhou. However, thanks to years of careful maintenance, these dove trees began to bloom in 2010 and have been blooming more profusely each year since.

Currently, the taller dove tree beside Longyue Pavilion on Lingfeng Hill, and the two slimmer ones next to the corridor opposite the lawn, are all in bloom. The Hangzhou Botanical Garden has successfully cultivated nearly a hundred dove tree seedlings. Visitors can now see blooming dove trees not only beside Longyue Pavilion but also in the plant classification area.

Interestingly, dove trees are quite particular about their location, for their neighbor is the over 100-year-old Qixing ancient wintersweet. It is said that the ancient wintersweet was planted by the monks of Lingfeng Temple during the Qing Dynasty. After a hundred years, only seven clumps of wintersweet remain, arranged like the seven stars of the Big Dipper (Qixing). They are especially renowned for their early blooming and late shedding of flowers. Today's Longyue Pavilion stands on the former site of Lingfeng Temple.

Before the Song Dynasty, Lingfeng Hill was known as Jiufeng Hill ("Vulture Hill"). Initially, this hill was renowned for its Buddhist temples rather than for its plum blossoms and dove trees. 1600 years ago, the Buddhist monk Huili brought Buddhism to Hangzhou and built five temples, including Lingyin and Lingfeng, around the Peak Flying from Afar. During the Kaiyun reign of the Later Jin Dynasty (944—947), the King of Wuyue built Jiufeng Zen Buddhist Temple here. In the second year of the Zhiping reign of Emperor Yingzong of the Northern Song Dynasty (1065), the emperor renamed the temple "Lingfeng Temple". Over time, Lingfeng Temple continued to flourish and became one of the most prestigious temples in Hangzhou. During the Song Dynasty, it was known as North Tianzhu, holding the same esteemed status as Lingyin Temple, which was referred to as West Tianzhu. However, while Lingyin Temple has consistently thrived, Lingfeng Temple has experienced periods of prosperity and decline.

During the reign of Emperor Daoguang (1821—1850), Gu Qing, vice commander-in-chief of the Hangzhou garrison, was captivated by the elegance and seclusion of Lingfeng Hill. As a result, he allocated funds to rebuild Lingfeng Temple and erected a stone stele titled "A Record of Rebuilding Lingfeng Temple beside West Lake". This stele still stands today in Juyue Pavilion within the Lingfeng scenic area.

During the Republic of China, Lingfeng Temple received few visitors and pilgrims due to its remote location. During the War of Resistance against Japanese Aggression, when Hangzhou fell, Lingfeng Temple collapsed, its monks scattered, and the once-thriving plum forest became desolate. By the early 1950s, the temple was left with nothing but broken walls, the Bowl Washing Pool, Juyue Spring, and Crane Luring Pavilion.

The antiqued Longyue Pavilion we see today was built in 1988 by the municipal landscape and forestry department.

冷泉溪畔的飞来峰造像
Cold Spring by Stone Carvings
of Peak Flying from Afar

灵隐飞来峰景区，冷泉亭

Cold Spring Pavilion at Lingyin Feilaifeng Scenic Area

1200 多岁的冷泉亭

冷泉亭 ●

飞来峰前，有一条清冽澄澈的溪流，叫北涧，也叫冷泉溪，是西湖的重要水源之一。冷泉溪边，立着一座冷泉亭，这是一个四角重檐歇山亭，斜对面就是灵隐寺山门。

每天都有五湖四海的游客来到这里，他们常会坐在亭内，听着溪水声歇脚。很多人可能不知道，这座亭子至今已经有 1200 多年历史，它是历代文人骚客流连忘返的地方。

让冷泉亭闻名天下的，是杭州"老市长"白居易的一篇《冷泉亭记》。如果没有这篇美文，后人可能不会知道这里还有这样一座风景绝美的亭子。《冷泉亭记》的落款时间为"长庆三年（823）八月十三日"，距今 1200 多年。

了解了冷泉亭的来历，你去灵隐飞来峰游玩的时候，会去认真看一看冷泉亭吗？

唐长庆二年（822）的秋天，白居易新任杭州刺史，刺史是一个地方的最高行政长官，相当于今天的市长。在唐代，共有 90 余人来杭州当过"市长"，其中有两位名声响亮，一位是李泌，另一位就是白居易。

白居易来杭州时已经 50 岁了，在杭州的这段日子，他四处游历，这里的湖山风光大大治愈了这位中年才子不得志的心。他写"忆江南，最忆是杭州"，又写"在郡六百日，入山十二回"，这里的"山"，即灵隐天竺一带，而在他眼中，最能抚平心绪的地方，便是飞来峰前的冷泉亭。

有一次，白居易来到冷泉亭前，想要修建一座刺史亭，不料被他的好友韬光法师劝阻。韬光法师告诉他，这里已有五座亭子了——冷泉亭由唐元和年间（806—820）杭州刺史元藇主持建造，在这之前，这一带还曾建有见山、虚白、观风、候仙四座亭子，它们合称"五亭"。

白居易认为韬光法师的话在理，如果亭子建得太多，反倒是煞风景了，但他还是忍不住在冷泉亭内留下墨宝，写下了"冷泉"二字。

那一晚回到府内，白居易仍对冷泉亭及周边的其他四亭久久难忘，于是，他不再执着于在溪水上造亭，而是把这种情感寄托于纸上，写下了著名的《冷泉亭记》："东南山水，余杭郡为最。就郡言，灵隐寺为尤。由寺观，冷泉亭为甲。亭在山下，水中央，寺西南隅……于是五亭相望，如指之列，可谓佳境殚矣，能事毕矣。后来者，虽有敏心巧目，无所加焉。故吾继之，述而不作。长庆三年，八月十三日记。"

白居易毫不吝惜自己的赞美之词，在这篇美文中，将视线一路聚焦在灵隐寺前的冷泉亭，认为这里的山水形胜为东南第一。他还交代了冷泉亭的建造背景，灵隐"五亭"是由历任官员分别建造的，冷泉亭最后建成。白居易给予五亭高度评价，认为"五亭相望，如指之列，可谓佳境殚矣，能事毕矣"，他作为"后来者"，"虽有敏心巧目，无所加焉"，于是选择了这种"述而不作"的方式。

虽然白居易不是冷泉亭的建造者，却是它的推广者，这篇亭记迅速在文化圈里火了，就此为冷泉亭成为一代名亭奠定了基础。

两百多年后，白居易的超级"迷弟"也慕名来到冷泉亭，他就是同样来杭州当"市长"的诗人官员苏轼。

苏轼号东坡居士，"东坡"这个名号与白居易有很深的渊源。白居易曾写过《东坡种花》《东坡种树》《别东坡种树》等诗篇。苏轼常在自己的诗作中表达对"偶像"白居易的仰慕。如他曾说："出处依稀似乐天，敢将衰朽校前贤"，"衰朽"是苏轼自喻，"前贤"就是指白居易。后来，他还给自己取了"东坡"

的雅号。

无论心境、思想，还是为官的执政理念等，苏东坡都与这位前辈有着高度重合的地方。白居易疏浚西湖，苏轼也疏浚西湖，他继承偶像的事业，并且将工程规模不断扩大。

白居易爱去的地方，苏轼自然也不肯错过。在看到白居易题写的"冷泉"二字匾额后，苏东坡情不自禁跟"偶像"完成了一次跨越时空的合作——提笔加上一个"亭"字，从此，世间有了"冷泉亭"。

爱屋及乌，苏东坡对冷泉亭的爱，比白居易更甚。他把办公室都直接"搬"到了亭子里。有史料为证，据南宋《梁溪漫志》记载："东坡镇余杭……以吏牍自随，至冷泉亭则据案剖决，落笔如风雨，分争辩讼，谈笑而办。已，乃与僚吏剧饮，薄晚则乘马以归。"

传说，苏东坡曾在冷泉亭"画扇判案"，判完案子，就开始就地喝酒吟诗。每次去时，必带上几个随从。一到亭子里，他便令牍吏摆上桌椅笔墨，摊开卷宗，开始判决公案。苏东坡豪放不羁，才思敏捷，工作效率很高。公务完毕，苏东坡就令人撤掉公文案卷，摆上酒菜，与手下牍吏共饮同酌；直到暮色降临，才恋恋不舍地打道回府。

在白居易和苏东坡的"名人效应"影响下，历代文人雅士只要到了灵隐，都会走进冷泉亭，跟随先贤"打卡"游赏。

明代书画家董其昌就是其中之一。他在冷泉亭留下了一副楹联："泉自何时冷起？峰自何处飞来？"

这种开放式提问的楹联，引得众多文人争相对仗。晚清名臣左宗棠曾题写过一副："在山本清，泉自源头冷起；入世皆幻，峰从天外飞来。"

后来，清末著名学者、一代经学大师俞樾跟夫人、女儿来飞来峰游玩的时候，也续了一联。俞樾写道："泉自有时冷起，峰从无处飞来。"俞夫人看了一眼，自己修改了一联："泉自冷时冷起，峰从飞处飞来。"女儿也跟着父母，续写了一联："泉自禹时冷起，峰从项处飞来。"

时光流逝，现在冷泉亭的匾额和对联都已经不是当年的了，但字迹仍在，这是一种文脉的传承。

今天我们看到的冷泉亭，并不在最早修建的位置。

唐代以后，冷泉亭于吴越宝大元年（924）经历了一次重建，建造情况无从考据，但据专家推测，当时的冷泉亭仍延续最早的样子，建在水中。

南宋是冷泉亭的又一次高光时刻。绍兴年间（1131—1162），人们对冷泉溪进行疏浚，并在冷泉亭附近建起石闸，蓄涧水。当池水暴涨时，就会开闸泄水，这时溪水奔涌，水花飞溅，人称"冷泉放闸"，诗人杨万里曾写"平地跳雪山，晴空下霹雳"，描写的就是这里的景象。

当时，飞来峰与冷泉亭还成了南宋皇家造园的灵感源泉。从帝王到王公贵族为什么独爱这里？这少不了白居易的推崇。

飞来峰仅高一百多米，这样的高度在园林叠山中既可以模仿，也容易接近，可游可登。而白居易一生清廉，在离任杭州前，别无他求，仅取了两片天竺石，并写了《丑石吟》记述此事。此外，他还在《太湖石记》中说"太湖为甲，罗浮、天竺之徒次焉"，他眼中的天竺石地位很高，仅次于太湖石。

在他强大的号召力影响下，历代文人墨客遍访此地。帝王们希望不用出城就可以欣赏杭州西湖美景，于是纷纷在自家园林中模仿西湖山水。最有名的，就是宋高宗在德寿宫内修建的"小西湖"，里面就仿建了飞来峰和冷泉亭。当年，从德寿宫遗址中挖出的"芙蓉石"，被乾隆皇帝收入北京圆明园，改名"青莲朵"。

到了明代，冷泉亭从水中移到了岸边，就是现在的位置。明代著名文学家袁宏道在万历二十五年（1597）游历杭州时，写道："灵隐寺在北高峰下，寺最奇胜，门景尤好。由飞来峰至冷泉亭一带，涧水溜玉，画壁流青，是山之极胜处。亭在山门外，尝读乐天记有云……观此记，亭当在水中。今依涧而立，涧阔不丈余，无可置亭者，然则冷泉之景，比旧盖减十分之七矣。"

袁宏道对白居易《冷泉亭记》所描绘的冷泉亭十分向往，慕名而来，但眼前看到的亭子并不在水中，水涧也不宽阔了。看来，"买家秀"和"卖家秀"相去甚远啊！

当然，爱它的人却将其视如宝藏。比如"西湖最强玩家"、明末著名文人张岱，就对重建后的冷泉亭情有独钟。他在《西湖梦寻·冷泉亭》中有生动的回忆："冷泉亭，在灵隐寺山门之左……亭对峭壁，一泓冷然，凄清入耳。亭后西栗十余株，大皆合抱，冷飔暗樾，遍体清凉。……夏月乘凉，移枕簟就亭中卧月……余在西湖，多在湖船作寓，夜夜见湖上之月；而今又避嚣灵隐，夜坐冷泉亭，又夜夜对山间之月。"张岱"强推"，这里是一个夏日乘凉、夜游的好去处。

到了清代，康熙南巡期间，将灵隐寺改名"云林寺"，并重修了冷泉亭。

在漫长的岁月中，灵隐"五亭"中的"虚白""候仙""观风""见山"四亭都已经淹没在时间的尘埃中，只有冷泉亭屡毁屡建。

冷泉亭
Cold Spring Pavilion

冷泉溪
Cold Spring

1200-Year-Old Cold Spring Pavilion

Cold Spring Pavilion

West Lake

In front of the Peak Flying from Afar, there is a fresh and cool stream called Beijian, also known as Cold Spring, which is one of the main water sources for West Lake. Beside the stream stands Cold Spring Pavilion, with its gable and hip roof featuring multiple eaves. It is diagonally opposite the gate of Lingyin Temple.

Every day, tourists from all over the world often stop here for a short rest, sitting in the pavilion and listening to the gurgling of the stream. To many people's surprise, with a history of over 1,200 years, this pavilion has been a gathering place for literati for generations.

The Pavilion became famous thanks to "A Record of Cold Spring Pavilion" written by Bai Juyi, the former "mayor" of Hangzhou. Without this record, future generations might not know about this picturesque pavilion. The inscription in "A Record of Cold Spring Pavilion" is dated "August 13th, the third year of the Changqing era" (823 CE), exactly 1,200 years ago.

After learning about the origin of Cold Spring Pavilion, when you visit the Peak Flying from Afar in Lingyin again, will you take a closer look at Cold Spring Pavilion?

In the fall of 822 CE, Bai Juyi was appointed governor of Hangzhou Prefecture, the top local administrator, equivalent to today's mayor. During the Tang Dynasty, over 90 people served as "mayor" of Hangzhou. Two of them are particularly famous: Li Bi and Bai Juyi.

Bai Juyi was 50 when he arrived in Hangzhou. During his time there, he traveled extensively, and the beautiful lakescape greatly healed the heart of this middle-aged, yet unfulfilled talent. He wrote in his poems "In my memories of Jiangnan, the most memorable is Hangzhou", and "During six hundred days in Hangzhou, I hiked into the mountains twelve times". The "mountains" refer to the areas around Lingyin and Tianzhu mountains. To him, the most soothing place was Cold Spring Pavilion in front of the Peak Flying from Afar.

One day, Bai Juyi visited Cold Spring Pavilion with plans to build a pavilion in the name of governor, but his good friend, Zen Master Taoguang, unexpectedly persuaded him otherwise. The master informed him that, besides Cold Spring Pavilion, constructed under Yuan Xu, the governor of Hangzhou during the Yuanhe era of the Tang Dynasty, four other pavilions had already been built in previous dynasties: Jianshan Pavilion, Xubai Pavilion, Guanfeng Pavilion, and Houxian Pavilion. Together, these were known as the "Five Pavilions".

Bai Juyi agreed with his friend that too many pavilions would spoil the scenery. However, he couldn't resist entering Cold Spring Pavilion to inscribe the characters "Cold Spring" in his calligraphy.

That night, back at home, Bai Juyi was preoccupied with thoughts of Cold Spring Pavilion and the other four pavilions. He decided against building a new pavilion by the stream and instead expressed his deep affinity with the pavilion in his famous prose, "A Record of Cold Spring Pavilion": "For the landscapes of southeast China, Hangzhou stands unrivaled. Within this prefecture, Lingyin Temple holds the crown for the finest scenery. And within the temple, Cold Spring Pavilion offers the most breathtaking view... Nestled at the mountain's base, surrounded by waters in the temple's southwest corner, it is a gem among five pavilions that complement each other like the fingers of a hand. Together, they create a flawless panorama, leaving little need for further landscaping. Even the most ingenious governors of future generations can add nothing to this perfection. Thus, as I assume the role of governor, my duty is to depict and preserve this landscape, not to build another pavilion to enhance it. August,13th, the third year of the Changqing era."

In his eloquent prose, he lavished praise without reservation, directing his admiration towards Cold Spring Pavilion before Lingyin Temple, deeming its landscape the finest in all of southeast China. In his prose, he offered a succinct yet evocative account of the construction history of Cold Spring Pavilion, particularly highlighting how the "five pavilions" of Lingyin were erected by successive prefects, culminating in the completion of Cold Spring Pavilion. Bai Juyi spoke highly of these five pavilions:

"five pavilions that complement each other like the fingers of a hand. Together, they create a flawless panorama, leaving little need for further landscaping." Although he was one of "the most ingenious governors of future generations", he chose to "depict and preserve this landscape, not to build another pavilion to enhance it".

Although Bai Juyi was not the builder of Cold Spring Pavilion, he was its promoter. His prose soon went viral in literary circles, paving the way for Cold Spring Pavilion to become the most prestigious pavilion of its era.

Over two hundred years later, Bai Juyi's super fan, the poet and official Su Shi, visited Cold Spring Pavilion in admiration of Bai Juyi when he became the "mayor" of Hangzhou.

Su Shi, also known as Dongpo Jushi, had a literary name "Dongpo" (meaning "the slope east of the city") that was deeply connected to Bai Juyi. Bai Juyi wrote poems like "Planting Flowers on the Eastern City Slope, Planting Trees on the Eastern City Slope", and "The Sequel to 'Planting Trees on the Eastern City Slope' ". Su Shi often expressed his admiration for his idol Bai Juyi in his own poems. For instance, in his poem "Heading to Hangzhou", he wrote, "My political life is similar to Letian's, so I dare to compare my aged and useless self to this former sage." The phrase "aged and useless" reflects Su Shi's self-effacing gesture, while "former sage" refers to Bai Juyi, whose courtesy name was Letian. Later, he adopted the literary name "Dongpo".

His mindset, thoughts, and philosophy of governing Hangzhou closely resembled those of his predecessor. Following Bai Juyi's example, he dredged West Lake, continuing his idol's work and expanding the project.

Bai Juyi's favorite spots naturally became Su Shi's favorites. After seeing Bai Juyi's "Cold Spring" plaque, Su Dongpo couldn't resist collaborating with his idol across time by adding the word "Pavilion". Thus, "Cold Spring Pavilion" came into existence.

Out of his admiration for Bai Juyi, Su Dongpo cherished Cold Spring Pavilion even more. He even "moved" his office directly to the pavilion. According to *Miscellaneous Records of Liangxi* during the Southern Song Dynasty, "While serving as Hangzhou's governor...Dongpo, accompanied by clerks, would immediately start handling litigation upon arriving at Cold Spring Pavilion. He swiftly and smoothly resolved disputes and lawsuits with ease. He would then drink with his subordinates until evening before riding home."

Legend has it that Su Dongpo once settled a lawsuit at Cold Spring Pavilion by drawing on fans, and then stayed to drink and recite poems on the spot. Every time he went there, he was accompanied by several attendants. Upon reaching the pavilion, he would have his clerks prepare his table, chair, pens, and ink, then start handling complaints and litigation. Su Dongpo was unrestrained, quick-witted, and highly efficient. After completing his official duties, he would have his table cleared of documents and bring out wine and food to drink with his subordinates until the evening, reluctantly heading home afterward.

Thanks to the "celebrity effect" of Bai Juyi and Su Dongpo, future literati made it a point to visit Cold Spring Pavilion whenever they toured Lingyin Mountain, following in the footsteps of these former sages.

Notably, the Ming Dynasty painter and calligrapher Dong Qichang stands out. He left a couplet in Cold Spring Pavilion: "When did the spring turn so cold? Where did the lofty peak fly from? "

This open-ended couplet attracted many literati to compete in answering it. Zuo Zongtang, a renowned minister of the late Qing Dynasty, once inscribed: "From the mountain where it originates, the spring turned cold; into the world of illusions, the peak flew from afar. "

Later, during the late Qing Dynasty, renowned scholar and Confucian Master Yu Yue, along with his wife and daughter, wrote another couplet while touring the Peak Flying from Afar. Yuyue wrote: "The spring turned cold sometime. The peak flew from nowhere." Perhaps Mrs. Yu was unsatisfied with his couplet, so she offered a revised version: "The spring turned cold when it was cold. The peak flew from where it flew from." Their daughter, inspired by her parents, added her own couplet: "The spring turned cold since the time of Da Yu, and the peak flew after being lifted by Xiang Yu. "

Although, after so many years, the plaque and couplet of Cold Spring Pavilion are not the originals and the inscriptions are gone, the words have been preserved as cultural heritage.

The Cold Spring Pavilion we see today is not in its original location.

After the Tang Dynasty, the pavilion was rebuilt in the first year of King Qian Liu's Baoda reign of the Wuyue State (924 CE). Its appearance after reconstruction is unknown, but experts speculate it was built in water, modeled after its original form.

The Cold Spring Pavilion regained popularity during the Southern Song Dynasty. During Emperor Gaozong's Shaoxing reign (1131–1162), Cold Spring was dredged and a stone water lock was built to store its water. When the water surged, the lock would be opened to release it. The rushing and splashing stream created a scene known as "Releasing Cold Spring from the Water Lock". Poet Yang Wanli described it perfectly "A snow-capped hill pops out of the ground and thunderbolts fall from the clear sky", capturing the magnificent spectacle.

At that time, the Peak Flying from Afar and Cold Spring Pavilion inspired the design of the Imperial Garden of the Southern Song Dynasty. Why did the emperors and nobles have such a unique affection for this place? It can all be attributed to Bai Juyi's advocacy.

The Peak Flying from Afar is only about a hundred meters tall, making it easy to replicate with a rockery. Its accessibility and appeal for hiking and touring made the imitation a popular scenic spot. Throughout his life, Bai Juyi was honest and upright. Before leaving Hangzhou, he asked for nothing but two stones from Tianzhu Mountain and wrote the poem "Ugly Stone Chant". In his prose "A Story of Taihu Ston", he noted, "The stones from Taihu Lake are the best, followed by those from Luofu Mountain and Tianzhu Mountain." To him, Tianzhu stones held a very high status, second only to Taihu stones.

Inspired by his strong advocacy, generations of literati visited this place. Emperors, wishing to enjoy the beauty of West Lake without traveling to Hangzhou, replicated its landscapes in their own gardens. The most famous garden is "Miniature West Lake", built in Deshou Palace by Emperor Gaozong of the Southern Song Dynasty, featuring imitations of the Peak Flying from Afar and Cold Spring Pavilion. The "Hibiscus Stone", unearthed from the ruins of Deshou Palace, was moved to the Yuanmingyuan (Old Summer Palace) by order of Emperor Qianlong and renamed "Blue Lotus Flower".

During the Ming Dynasty, Cold Spring Pavilion was relocated from the water to its current position beside the bank. In 1597, while traveling in Hangzhou, Yuan Hongdao, a renowned Ming Dynasty litterateur, wrote: "At the foot of the Northern Peak, Lingyin Temple boasts the most marvelous scenery, especially around its gate. In the area from the Peak Flying from Afar to Cold Spring Pavilion, the clear stream flows slowly like congealed jade, and the verdant hill walls covered with vines resemble dynamic paintings. This is where the best hillscape resides. Cold Spring Pavilion stands outside the temple's gate. I once read a travelogue by Letian...It states that the pavilion should be in the water. Now, standing by the stream, which is just over a zhang (approximately 313 meters) wide, I see no pavilion in the stream. Today's Cold Spring Pavilion is 30% inferior to the original. "

Yuan Hongdao, inspired by Bai Juyi's "A Record of Cold Spring Pavilion", visited the pavilion, only to find it no longer in the water and the stream much narrower. Alas, seeing it for himself was better than hearing about it repeatedly.

Of course, its enthusiasts still cherish it as a treasure. For example, Zhang Dai, a famous late Ming Dynasty literatus known as "the No.1 traveler of West Lake", was obsessed with the rebuilt Cold Spring Pavilion. He vividly recounted his memories in the chapter "Cold Spring Pavilion" from his book *Search for West Lake in Dreams*: "Cold Spring Pavilion is located to the left of Lingyin Temple's gate. The pavilion, opposite the cliffs, stands beside a clear, cold spring, murmuring and desolate. West of the pavilion, there are about ten chestnut trees, each wide enough to be fully embraced by a man. They provide cool shade, which refreshes people's whole bodies... On moonlit summer nights, you can move your bedding to the pavilion and sleep there to enjoy the coolness... When I tour West Lake, I usually stay on a boat to enjoy the moonlit lake every night. Now, to escape the hustle and bustle, I rest in Cold Spring Pavilion on Lingyin Mountain, where I can enjoy the moonscape among the mountains." Zhang Dai strongly recommended this pavilion as the perfect place to enjoy the coolness of summer nights and for night tours.

During the Qing Dynasty, Emperor Kangxi renamed Lingyin Temple "Yunlin Temple" and rebuilt Cold Spring Pavilion during his southern tour.

Over the years, four of the "Five Pavilions of Lingyin"—Xubai, Houxian, Guanfeng, and Jianshan—have faded into history. Only Cold Spring Pavilion has repeatedly undergone destruction and reconstruction.

深秋晨曦中的灵隐寺
Lingyin Temple in Late Autumn
Awakened by Daylight

避暑胜地云栖竹径

西湖

云栖竹径

炎炎夏日，想要不离开杭州，寻一处避暑的清静地，绿荫环绕的云栖竹径是不错的选择。

这里曾是古代皇家来西湖周边游览必打卡的一站。康熙、乾隆都十分中意这座植物"秘密花园"，频频出入，还走出了一条"御道"。

不过，对于很多杭州人来说，云栖竹径多少还是有点冷门的。有人是只听过没去过，抑或去爬五云山而匆匆路过。

倒是在它对面的茶田里有一棵"孤独的树"，最近几年走红网络。因为这棵树孤零零立在整片茶园中间，一年四季都有人来拍它，"孤独的树"不算孤独，一路之隔的云栖才是真正的幽静处。

云栖竹径位于西湖的西南边，在钱塘江北岸的五云山云栖坞里。

相传五云山上常有五彩祥云在坞中栖留，并经久不散，滋养了这里的草木万物，因而得名"云栖"，又因为万千茂竹、曲径通幽，所以得名云栖竹径。

吴越时期，这里曾有著名佛寺"云栖寺"。《清一统志·杭州府二》记载，云栖寺"吴越建。宋治平二年改名栖真禅院。后废"。明隆庆五年（1571），掘地得碑，即古云栖寺。清康熙三十八年（1699），康熙帝在云栖御题"云栖"

及"松云间"两额。

两年后，康熙帝再次到了云栖寺，赐名寺前一竿大竹为"皇竹"，总督梁鼐就此建了"皇竹亭"。乾隆十六年（1751），乾隆帝又在云栖御题"香门净土""悦性亭""修篁深处"三额。乾隆二十七年（1762），他再在云栖御题"西方极乐世界安养道场"额。

两位皇帝如此偏爱的地方，自然名声在外。当时的云栖竹径叫"云栖梵径"，被列为西湖十八景之一。1985年，云栖竹径景区被评为"西湖新十景之首"。

主干道中间为米色平整石板，两侧用小碎石砌，在碎石和石板之间用黑砖镶出两道黑线，黑线以内过去是专供皇帝游景漫步而特意铺设的御道，当年康熙皇帝巡游云栖，也曾沿着此路上山。

一路上，两侧竹茂林密，高大挺拔的竹子直插云霄。官方数据显示，云栖景区占地面积150亩，其中竹林面积就达120亩左右，主要品种有大黄苦竹、紫竹、毛竹、方竹、凤尾竹、黄金嵌玉等。这里被称为"天然氧吧"，很适合漫步怡情。

径直往里走大概两三分钟，会见到一座亭。这座亭的名字很适合想要短暂逃离焦躁的都市人——"洗心亭"，取自佛教所强调的心境澄净。

亭前还有一方泉池——洗心池。亭柱还留有一副对联："翠滴千竿遮径竹，寒生六月洗心泉。"即便是在35℃以上的高温天，到了这里，暑气也会消散掉一些。景区工作人员曾做过测量，夏季高温天下午1点左右，洗心亭附近的温度比景区入口的马路低5℃左右。

再往前，依次是景碑亭、回龙亭、双碑亭等景点。蜿蜒深入，竹子的数量开始逐渐减少，取而代之的是古树群落。沿云栖竹径一路向上可以通往五云山顶，虽然不算陡峭，但台阶较多，相对来说比较消耗体力；再顺着五云山下山，可以到九溪。

云栖竹径，还拥有大量自然宝藏——满园子的古树名木。

2023年，浙江省林业局发布第一批省古树名木文化公园认定名单，云栖竹径枫香古树文化公园被评为"省古树名木文化公园"，是一座天然的古树名木博物馆。

云栖的地理环境得天独厚，不但有修篁蔽天，而且古木成荫。西湖树龄、体量名列前茅的古树，多半集中在这里。

山顶那棵树龄近 1500 年的老银杏高 20 多米，树干大过 12 座的圆台面，它被称为"浙江省十大最美银杏"之一。

半山腰双碑亭旁，有 3 棵寿逾 1040 年的枫香树，其中 1 棵主干高达 38 米，粗壮可容 3 人合抱。站在树干下仰视，可见它势干云表，高不可攀。

这些古老的树木见证了西湖湖光山色千年的历史行迹。

不仅如此，杭州市共有 5 棵名木，其中 2 棵香樟树就在云栖，它们是陈云同志在 1987 年亲手栽种的，如今已亭亭如盖。陈云同志十分青睐云栖，曾 30 多次到云栖，他总是遇山门而下车，策杖而行，徜徉石阶竹径，乐在其中。

云栖竹径还是杭州城区内拥有古树名木最多的公园，古树名木多达 120 株，涵盖枫香、苦槠、糙叶树、樟树、豹皮樟、槐、浙江楠、红果榆等 17 个树种。其中树龄千年以上的就有 4 株，以枫香古树数量最多，共有 49 株，还生长着杭州最美古树群——浙江楠古树群。

最近几年，云栖竹径枫香古树文化公园内都会举办杭州市古树名木主题展。内容翔实的宣传展板就分布在云栖竹径整个公园中，主要展示杭州市古树名木文化故事、古树名木保护优秀案例以及发展历程等。市民游客能近距离观察古老而珍贵的"活化石"，感受穿越千年的绿色底蕴，同时公园也能借此倡导全民参与保护。

云栖竹径
Yunqi Bamboo Grove Trail

洗心亭
Xixin Pavilion

Yunqi Bamboo Grove Trail: Summer Oasis

West Lake

Yunqi Bamboo Grove Trail

In the hot summer, if you're looking for a quiet escape in Hangzhou from the heat, the Yunqi Bamboo Grove Trail, surrounded by greenery, is a great choice.

This place was once the most must-see spot on any ancient imperial tour of West Lake. Emperors Kangxi and Qianlong were so captivated by this "secret botanical garden" that they visited frequently, turning the well-trodden path into an "imperial path".

However, for many locals in Hangzhou, the Yunqi Bamboo Grove Trail remains relatively unknown. Some people have heard of it but never visit it, while others simply pass by it when hiking up Wuyun Mountain.

In contrast, a "solitary tree" in the tea field opposite it has gone viral online in recent years. Despite standing alone in the middle of the tea garden, the "solitary tree" attracts tourists year-round for photos and is far from solitary. Just a road away, the Yunqi Bamboo Grove Trail remains a truly isolated spot.

The Yunqi Bamboo Grove Trail is situated southwest of West Lake, in Yunqi Col, next to Wuyun Mountain on the north bank of the Qiantang River.

Legend has it that Wuyun Mountain was once capped with colorful clouds that lingered in the col for a long time, nourishing the grass and trees. This is why the place was named "Yunqi" ("where clouds linger"). The trail, lined with thousands of lush bamboo, is known as the Yunqi Bamboo Grove Trail.

During the Wuyue period, this area was home to the famous Buddhist temple, Yunqi Temple. According to "Records of Hangzhou Prefecture (Volume 2)" in *Annals of the Qing Dynasty*, Yunqi Temple "was built during the Wuyue period and later, during the second year of Emperor Yingzong's Zhiping reign, it was renamed Qizhen Zen Buddhist Temple. Eventually, it was abolished". In the fifth year of Emperor Muzong's Longqing reign (1571) during the Ming Dynasty, a stone stele was unearthed, marking the original site of Yunqi Temple. In the 38th year of Emperor Kangxi's reign (1699), the emperor inscribed the words "Yun Qi" ("where clouds linger") and "Song Yun Jian" ("among pines and clouds") on two plaques.

Two years later, Emperor Kangxi revisited Yunqi Temple and named a large bamboo in front of the temple "Huangzhu" ("imperial bamboo"). Governor Liang Nai then built the "Huangzhu Pavilion" to commemorate it. In the 16th year of Emperor Qianlong's reign (1751), the emperor visited and inscribed three plaques with the words "Xiang Men Jing Tu" ("pure land beside a temple"), "Yue Xing Ting" ("mental delighting pavilion"), and "Xiu Huang Shen Chu" ("deep behind slender bamboos"). In the 27th year of Emperor Qianlong's reign (1762), the emperor inscribed another plaque with the words "Seat of Resting in the Land of Bliss".

Since two emperors frequented this place, the Yunqi Bamboo Grove Trail (originally "Yunqi Buddhist Trail") has become so renowned that it is now listed as one of the 18 sights of West Lake. In 1985, the Yunqi Bamboo Grove Trail was ranked first among the new ten sights of West Lake.

The main road is made of beige flat stones with small gravel on both sides. Black bricks mark two lines between the stones and gravel, creating a path reserved for emperors' tours. When Emperor Kangxi visited Yunqi, he used this imperial road to hike up the mountain.

Follow this trail, and you'll be enchanted by dense, green groves of tall, sky-reaching bamboos on both sides. Official data show that the Yunqi scenic area covers 150 *mu*, with approximately 120 *mu* dedicated to bamboo forests. The area is home to about ten main varieties of bamboo, including Oligostachyum sulcatum, black bamboo, tortoise shell bamboo, square bamboo, fernleaf bamboo, and Phyllostachys aureosulcata. This place is known as the "natural oxygen bar", making it perfect for strolling and sightseeing.

Walk straight for about two to three minutes, and you'll come across a pavilion. The name of this pavilion is ideal for those looking to escape the hustle and bustle of city life for a short while. It's called Xixin Pavilion ("mind-cleaning pavilion"), a name inspired by the Buddhist concept of purifying the mind.

In front of the pavilion, there is a spring-fed pond called Xixin Pond ("mind-cleansing pond"). A couplet is inscribed on the pavilion's pillars: Thousands of green bamboo groves conceal the trail, June's cool spring cleans minds, without fail. Even on a hot day over 35°C, the summer heat seems to dissipate a bit when you arrive here. According to measurements taken by the scenic area staff, on hot summer days around 1:00 p.m., the temperature around Xixin Pavilion is 5°C lower than that of the highway at the entrance to the scenic area.

Continue walking, and you will pass Jingbei Pavilion, Huilong Pavilion, Double Stele Pavilion, and other attractions. As the trail winds deeper, the number of bamboos gradually decreases, giving way to ancient trees. The Yunqi Bamboo Grove Trail leads all the way to the top of Wuyun Mountain. Although the trail isn't steep, the numerous steps make it relatively more physically demanding. From the top of Wuyun Mountain, you can hike down to reach Jiuxi Creeks.

The Yunqi Bamboo Grove Trail also boasts a wealth of natural treasures, including a garden filled with ancient and renowned trees.

In 2023, the Forestry Bureau of Zhejiang Province released the first batch of provincial ancient and famous trees cultural park identification list. The "Yunqi Bamboo Grove Trail" Chinese Sweetgum Cultural Park was recognized as a provincial cultural park of ancient and famous trees, serving as a natural museum.

Yunqi, blessed with a unique geographic environment, boasts not only towering, slender bamboos but also a lush garden of ancient trees. This area is home to the oldest and largest ancient trees in the West Lake scenic region.

For example, at the top of Wuyun Mountain, there is a ginkgo tree that is nearly 1,500 years old and over 20 meters tall, with a trunk larger than a 12-seat round table. It is known as the one of the "top ten most beautiful ginkgos in Zhejiang".

Halfway up Wuyun Mountain, next to Double Stele Pavilion, there are three Chinese sweetgum trees, each over 1,040 years old. One of them has a trunk that is 38 meters tall and wide enough for three people to encircle. Standing beneath it and looking up, you will feel as if it reaches the sky, beyond the reach of mortals.

These ancient trees have witnessed the history of West Lake's landscape for a millennium.

Significantly, Hangzhou boasts five famous trees, two of which are camphor trees located in Yunqi. These were planted by Chen Yun, Chairman of the Central Advisory Commission, in 1987. Now, they stand there with graceful poise, their tops spreading out with exuberant foliage. Chen Yun was very fond of Yunqi, visiting it more than 30 times. At the entrance, he would always get out of his vehicle and walk in with a cane, taking delight in wandering along the trail through the bamboo groves.

The Yunqi Bamboo Grove Trail area is the park in Hangzhou's urban area with the most ancient and famous trees—specifically, as many as 120. These trees include 17 varieties, such as Chinese sweetgum, Castanopsis sclerophylla, Aphananthe aspera, camphor, Litsea coreana var. sinensis, Sophora japonica, Phoebe chekiangensis, and Ulmus szechuanica. Among them, there are four trees that are over a thousand years old. The park contains the largest number of Chinese sweetgum trees, totaling 49, and also showcases the most beautiful ancient tree group in Hangzhou—the Phoebe chekiangensis group.

In recent years, the themed exhibition of Hangzhou's ancient and famous trees has been held at the "Yunqi Bamboo Grove Trail" Chinese Sweetgum Cultural Park. Detailed information panels are placed throughout the park, showcasing the cultural stories of Hangzhou's ancient and famous trees, exemplary preservation cases, and the history of their conservation efforts. Citizens and tourists can get close to these ancient and precious "living fossils", experience the green heritage that spans millennia. The park also promote widespread participation in their protection.

云栖竹径
Yunqi Bamboo Trail

云栖竹径对面茶田里；有一棵 "孤独的树"
The "Solitary Tree" in the Tea Field Opposite
the Yunqi Bamboo Grove Trail

西湖"香灰泥"堆出江洋畈

● 江洋畈生态公园

北宋元祐四年（1089），52 岁的苏轼第二次来杭州做官，职务是杭州知府、龙图阁学士。一上任，他就干了一件大事——疏浚西湖。

为什么要疏浚西湖？西湖是自然形成的潟湖（xì hú），周围山上的溪流把淡水和泥沙带入湖中，天长日久，这些泥沙不断堆积，容易把西湖堵塞，要保持湖水的深度，必须经常挖泥疏浚。

自唐代以来，西湖的疏浚工作就一直在进行中。古代规模较大的西湖疏浚有五次，除了由宋代"市长"苏轼主导之外，之前有唐代的白居易，之后有明代杨孟瑛以及清代的李卫和阮元组织进行。

白堤、苏堤、杨公堤、阮公墩等杭州人熟悉的景点，都是由西湖疏浚出来的淤泥堆积而成的。一次次疏浚，奠定了西湖的千年繁华。如果没有历代的疏通、挖深和整理，也许西湖早已变成了田荡。

1949 年后，西湖进行了三次规模庞大的疏浚，分别是 1951 年至 1958 年，1976 年至 1982 年，以及最近的一次，1999 年至 2003 年。西湖的水深，也从 0.55 米到 1.8 米，再到今天的 2.27 米。

西湖湖底的浮泥层和软泥层，俗称"香灰泥"，含有丰富的氮、磷等营养成分，在水中释放，对西湖水质的影响很大。

从西湖中挖出的"香灰泥"富有营养，若用于种植草木，很容易形成一处生机勃勃的自然天地。这些年，从湖底清挖出来的淤泥，成就了一处新的美景——江洋畈生态公园。

江洋畈的美，必须身临其境，才能深有体会。

江洋畈的名字，出自《南宋书》，距今已经有 1500 年的历史。

江洋，即钱塘江；畈，意思是大片的田地。曾经的江洋畈，一直是江海退去后留下来的一片普普通通的滩涂，随着时间推移，江洋畈区域慢慢缩小。现在的江洋畈面积为 19.8 公顷，约合 300 亩。

1999 年，西湖疏浚清挖出 100 万方淤泥，被输送堆积到江洋畈。在这些淤泥里沉睡了数百年的水生、陆生植物种子，也渐渐苏醒、孕育、发芽。

今天的江洋畈，经过多年的堆晒、蓄力与酝酿，厚积薄发，无为而治，还原出了水生湿地自然演替的本真模样。

即便知名度逐年提高，这里依旧是杭州的冷门景点。喜欢它的人很喜欢，把这里看作是一个私藏秘境，不喜欢的人则一脸疑惑："这个淤泥堆出来的公园，到底有什么好玩的？"

来了就知道了。它地处玉皇山南麓，离南宋皇城大遗址很近，原先是钱王山、大慈山之间的山间谷地。四周的山脉仿佛是一道天然屏障，为江洋畈隔绝了闹市的喧嚣。

江洋畈生态公园的主入口在山腰上，需要爬一段坡。一进门，瞬间就被葱茏的绿意包围。这里一直以"最小干预"为原则，顺其自然发展，完整地保留了原生态植被，即便是后来补种上去的植物，也全部选用原生品种：金鸡菊、狼尾草、红蓼、接骨木、波斯菊等。

曾有人打比方，说江洋畈很像是西湖"后宫"里一位不争不骄的妃子，不施粉黛，也无需滤镜。

来到这里，你会发现，原来这种宁静中带点洒脱的美，才最撩人。

正门右手边枕霞廊南侧的坡面上，齐刷刷地开了成片的大花金鸡菊。它没有牡丹雍容华贵，也不像正值盛花期的绣球花绚烂丰富，但你会忍不住对它"拍、拍、拍"。不过金鸡菊的花期很短，最佳观赏期是六月上旬。

在江洋畈，有很多植物都是从西湖淤泥里的原始种子孕育而来，像南川柳、旱柳、接骨草等。其中，最先长出来又最特别的，就是南川柳。

走在木栈道上，总有一簇簇细小的柳絮迎面飘来，但环顾四周也没有发现附近有垂柳。一棵棵树找过去，才发现了正在飘絮的南川柳。

这是一种生命力很顽强的落叶乔木，非常耐水湿。它的枝叶不像西湖边的垂柳一样垂下，而是向空中伸展，叶子也比垂柳宽大一点。

南川柳曾经在西湖边生长，但随着时间推移，南川柳被垂柳代替，如今的西湖边已经看不到它们的身影了。但是，南川柳的种子落进西湖，被深深埋进湖底的淤泥中，经疏浚工程来到了江洋畈。

在阳光雨露的滋润下，消失多年的西湖南川柳机缘巧合地在几千米外的江洋畈焕发了新的生机。据钱江管理处工作人员介绍，现在公园中最古老的南川

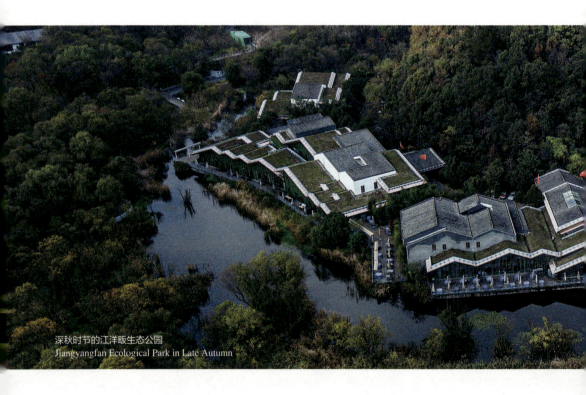

深秋时节的江洋畈生态公园
Jiangyangfan Ecological Park in Late Autumn

柳的种子，曾经在西湖底沉睡了六百余年。

处处是生机的江洋畈，当然不只有植物，动物们也都纷纷来这里落户。

这里有成片的芦苇荡，芦苇也是江洋畈主要的植物之一。芦苇是一种生命力很顽强的植物，最高能长到 6 米。喜欢往里头钻的湿地鸟类，比如黑水鸡、野水鸭、白鹭，一个个都把家搬了过来。

整个公园设置了近 90 块科普牌，分别科普了江洋畈中动植物的相关内容，很适合家长带小朋友来边游玩边学习。

除了游玩，这里还有好吃的。江洋畈边上，就是杭帮菜博物馆，通常这两个地方是连起来逛的。很少有城市会为它自己的菜系建一个博物馆，但爱吃的杭州人，做到了。杭帮菜博物馆是目前中国最大的地方菜博物馆，占地 9 亩多，建筑面积 12470 平方米，分为展示陈列馆和三个可以吃上地道杭帮菜的餐厅。

深秋时节的江洋畈生态公园
An Aerial View of Jiangyangfan Ecological Park in Late Autumn

江洋畈生态公园，醉霞坡上大花金鸡菊盛开
Full-Bloomed Coreopsis drummondii Torr. et Gray on Zuixia Slope, Jiangyangfan

江洋畈生态公园，游览栈道
The Touring Boardway, Jiangyangfan Ecological Park

江洋畈生态公园，游览栈道
The Touring Boardwalk at Jiangyangfan Ecological Park

蒲秀湖
Puxiu Lake

West Lake "Incense-Ash Mud" Revitalizes Jiangyangfan

West Lake

Jiangyangfan

In 1089, at the age of 52, Su Shi returned to Hangzhou as its governor and Scholar of Longtu Pavilion. Upon taking office, he undertook a major project: dredging West Lake.

Why did he make that decision? West Lake is a naturally occurring lagoon. In other words, streams from the surrounding mountains often carry fresh water and sediment into the lake, causing it to gradually fill up with accumulated sediments. To maintain the lake's depth, dredging is necessary.

In fact, West Lake has been dredged continuously since the Tang Dynasty. Historically, West Lake has undergone large-scale dredging five times. Besides Su Shi, the "mayor" of Hangzhou during the Song Dynasty, Bai Juyi of the Tang Dynasty, Yang Mengying of the Ming Dynasty, and Li Wei and Ruan Yuan of the Qing Dynasty also led efforts to dredge the lake.

Many scenic spots well-known to Hangzhou locals, including Baidi Causeway, Sudi Causeway, Yanggong Causeway, and Ruangong Islet, are all made from dredged silt from West Lake. Repeated dredging over the centuries has laid the foundation for the enduring prosperity of West Lake. Without these successive generations of dredging, deep digging, and meticulous organization, West Lake might have long ago turned into a swampy field.

West Lake has been extensively dredged three times since 1949: first from 1951 to

1958, then from 1976 to 1982, and most recently from 1999 to 2003. The depth of West Lake has increased over time, from 0.55 meters to 1.8 meters, and to 2.27 meters now.

The floating mud layer and soft mud layer at the bottom of West Lake, commonly known as "incense-ash mud", are rich in nitrogen, phosphorus, and other nutrients. When released into the water, they significantly impact the water quality of West Lake.

The "incense-ash mud" is rich in nutrients, once removed from West Lake, and used for planting vegetation, it can easily foster a vibrant natural ecosystem. Over the years, the silt dredged from the bottom of the lake has given rise to a new scenic spot: Jiangyangfan Ecological Park.

The beauty of Jiangyangfan can only be truly appreciated through physical presence.

The name "Jiangyangfan" originates from Book of *The Southern Song Dynasty*, which dates back 1,500 years. The word "Jiangyang" refers to the Qiantang River, while the word "fan" literally means a large expanse of field. Jiangyangfan used to be an ordinary mudflat left behind by the receding river and sea. Over time, the area of Jiangyangfan has gradually shrunk. The current Jiangyangfan spans an area of 19.8 hectares, or approximately 300 *mu*.

In 1999, one million cubic meters of silt were dredged from West Lake and transported to be piled up at Jiangyangfan. Hidden in this silt, seeds of aquatic and terrestrial plants that had been dormant for hundreds of years have gradually awakened and begun to germinate.

After years of accumulation, storage, and natural development, today's Jiangyangfan has restored the natural succession of aquatic wetlands to its original state.

Despite its increasing popularity each year, this place remains at the top of the least-sightworthy list of scenic attractions in Hangzhou. Those who are fans of it truly worship it as a hidden dreamland. Those who aren't are puzzled, "It's just a park made from silt. What's so interesting about it? "

Just come and see for yourself. Jiangyangfan is situated at the southern foot of Yuhuang Hill, near the ruins of the Southern Song Imperial City. It was originally a valley between Qianwang Hill and Daci Hill. The surrounding hills act as a natural barrier, isolating Jiangyangfan from the hustle and bustle of the downtown area.

To reach the main entrance of Jiangyangfan Ecological Park, located on the hillside, you need to hike up a short distance. Upon entering, you'll be immediately surrounded by lush greenery. The principle of "minimal intervention" has always been effectively applied here, allowing for natural development. The original vegetation has been preserved intact, and even the plants that have been replanted since are all native species, such as Coreopsis drummondii Torr. et Gray, Pennisetum alopecuroides (L.) Spreng., Persicaria orientalis (L.) Spach, Sambucus williamsii Hance, Cosmos bipinnatus Cav.

Jiangyangfan is often compared to a concubine in the "imperial harem" of West Lake: she does not compete for attention or boast about herself, nor does she need to put on any makeup or use beauty filters.

When you're here, you'll find that this serene beauty, tinged with a sense of carefreeness, is the most captivating.

On the right side of the main entrance, on the southern slope of Zhenxia Corridor, large clusters of Coreopsis drummondii Torr. et Gray are in full bloom. It may not be as elegant as the peony, nor as showy as the hydrangea in full bloom, but you can't help but take pictures of it. However, the blooming period of Coreopsis drummondii Torr. et Gray is very short, with the best viewing time in early June.

In Jiangyangfan, many plants were cultivated from the original seeds found in the silt of West Lake, such as Salix rosthornii Seemen, Chinese willow, and Sambucus javanica Reinw. ex Blume. Among them, the first to grow and the most unique is the Salix rosthornii Seemen.

When walking along the plank path, you'll often feel wisps of willow catkin brushing against your face, yet you won't see any weeping willows nearby. After inspecting tree after tree, you will eventually find the Salix rosthornii Seemen, which is the source of the catkins.

This is a highly resilient deciduous tree, extremely resistant to water and moisture. Unlike the weeping willows by West Lake, its branches extend upwards into the air, and its leaves are broader.

The Salix rosthornii Seemen once grew by West Lake, but over time, it was replaced by the weeping willow and is no longer seen there. However, its seeds fell into West Lake, became buried in the silt at the bottom, and eventually resurfaced in Jiangyangfan after the lake was dredged.

Nourished by sunshine and rain, the Salix rosthornii Seemen, extinct by West Lake for years, unexpectedly revived in Jiangyangfan, a few kilometers away. According to the Qianjiang Management Office staff, the oldest seed in the park had been dormant at the bottom of West Lake for over six centuries.

Indeed, the vibrant Jiangyangfan is home to both diverse plant clusters and numerous animals.

Reeds, one of the main plants in Jiangyangfan, grow in large clusters. These resilient plants can grow up to 6 meters tall. Wetland birds like common moorhens, wild ducks, and egrets, which enjoy nesting in them, have gradually made their homes here.

The park features nearly 90 plaques that provide scientific information about the plants and animals in Jiangyangfan, making it an excellent place to visit and learn with children.

In addition to enjoying the visual delights of the park, tourists can also indulge in a real feast at the nearby restaurants. Next to Jiangyangfan is the Hangzhou Cuisine Museum. They often visit both the park and the museum in one trip. Few cities have a museum dedicated to their cuisine, but food-loving Hangzhou does. The Hangzhou Cuisine Museum is the largest local cuisine museum in China. The museum spans over 9 mu and has a construction area of 12,470 square meters. It features a display gallery and three dining halls where visitors can enjoy authentic Hangzhou dishes.

江洋畈生态公园，香菇草和狐尾藻
Clusters of Marsh Pennywort and Whorled Water-
Milfoil, Jiangyangfan

江洋畈生态公园
Jiangyangfan Ecological Park

杭帮菜博物馆
Hangzhou Cuisine Museum

梧桐不仅报秋，
还象征祥瑞

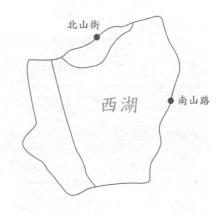

　　每年进入 11 月中下旬，一句经典文案就该上线了：杭州的秋天像打翻了的颜料盘，五彩斑斓。

　　杭州的秋天是真的美啊！尤其遇到连晴的日子，明媚的阳光洒在路边的树叶上，光影变幻。银杏、无患子、枫香、乌桕、鸡爪槭，黄、绿、赤、橙杂糅交错，特别好看。

　　但要说哪种树叶最能代表秋天，梧桐当仁不让。

　　梧桐跟秋天相连，自古有之。有个成语叫"一叶知秋"，出自西汉《淮南子·说山训》，很多人认为，那指的就是梧桐叶，因为梧桐是落叶大乔木，夏末季节就开始凋零，它的变色飘落，被认为是一种秋天的信号。

　　到了南宋，"梧桐报秋"更是成为一种高规格的宫廷仪式，梧桐是官方权威认证的"秋天代言人"。

　　宋代《梦粱录》里就有这样的记载，说的是，在立秋交节的时辰，太史官会穿着隆重的礼服，手持朝笏（hù），抑扬顿挫地奏报："秋来了！"这时候，梧桐叶也是给足面子，应声飞落一两片，以寓报秋意。

　　梧桐在古时地位高，不只起到报秋的作用，还是祥瑞的象征。

《庄子·秋水》中说："鹓鶵发于南海而飞于北海，非梧桐不止。"梧桐向阳而生，长势繁茂，人们视它为吉祥的象征，能引来凤凰啼鸣。在中国传统文化中，凤凰是什么样的存在？它是传说中的祥瑞神鸟，被誉为"百鸟之王"。梧桐能让高贵的凤凰都停下脚步栖息，地位自然是低不了的。

在许多古诗文里，凤凰和梧桐经常一起出现。于是，从前的皇宫或富贵殷实人家，常在庭院里栽种梧桐，不仅因为梧桐高大挺拔有气势，也因为有梧桐引凤凰的传说，寓意吉祥。

很多人不知道的是，报秋的梧桐，跟今天我们在北山街、南山路上看到的"梧桐"，其实是完全不同的两种植物，你甚至可能都没见过真正的梧桐。

古时的梧桐，属于梧桐科，叫中国梧桐，又叫青桐。它高大魁梧，树干挺直，树叶和枝干都是青绿色，树皮平滑翠绿，不长节。

而北山街、南山路上的"梧桐"，很多人叫它"法国梧桐"，本名是二球悬铃木，属于悬铃木科。它们不像中国梧桐那样"注重身材管理"，树干通常比较粗壮，容易长歪。树皮是片状剥落，老树皮剥落后会透出青白色的新树皮。

杭州的法国梧桐，也不是真的来自法国。17世纪，在英国牛津，人们用一球悬铃木（又叫美国梧桐）和三球悬铃木（又叫法国梧桐）作亲本，杂交成二球悬铃木，取名"英国梧桐"。在欧洲广泛栽培后，法国人把它带到中国作为行道树，人们就叫它"法国梧桐"。

二球悬铃木长得粗壮，树龄也长，在杭州的行道树中数量最多，占40%以上。它们适应性强、生长快，而且夏季有浓荫，冬季能落叶透阳，因而成了杭州行道树的首选。据杭州市园林文物局绿化处不完全统计，杭州市全市行道树中，目前悬铃木的种植数量有4.2万余株。

另一个原因是，中国梧桐的树冠是圆卵形，不算大，而悬铃木树冠硕大，枝叶繁茂，夏季遮阴，秋季观叶，冬季透光效果好。优胜劣汰，因此悬铃木被誉为"行道树之王"，而中国梧桐的知名度就要小得多。

有人会说，悬铃木万般好，但春天的飞絮也让人恼。

从2019年开始，园林绿化部门通过给树干注药的方式对梧桐飞絮加以抑制。通过树干螺旋给药，可以让植株受药更均衡，也可以帮助植物更好地吸收和分解药物,从而实现更好的抑制效果。近两年,还专门种植了一批少果悬铃木,这个品种的悬铃木,少结甚至不结球果,是一个"不飞毛"的悬铃木新品种。

秋末初冬,北山街、南山路上的悬铃木会更好看。当你去户外赏秋的时候,不妨也去找一找这座城市里的中国梧桐,毕竟它们才是真正的"梧桐树"。

那么,今天的杭州城里,还有哪些地方能看到中国梧桐?

杭州市园文局绿化处的专家说,梧桐在杭州种植较少,很多是 20 世纪 90 年代在单位附属绿地种植的,公共绿地应用不多。几年前,他们专门做过一次统计,整个杭州城的中国梧桐,一共 259 棵,种植最多的地方在中河南路,有 172 棵,这里也是杭州目前唯一一条以中国梧桐为行道树的道路。其他则是零星分布,我们在朝晖小区、劳动路、将军路、吴山路、海潮路、孝子坊都可以看到中国梧桐。

还有一个有趣的说法,说中国梧桐不仅能知秋,还能"知闰"。据说它每条枝上,平年生 12 叶,一边有 6 叶,而在闰年,则生 13 叶。这当然是没有科学依据的,只是偶然的巧合,但这赋予了梧桐树浪漫诗意的一面。

那么,如此被古人重视的中国梧桐,为什么后来没有在杭州普遍种植呢?

当然是有原因的。最主要的一个原因是病虫害多。梧桐树上有一种叫青桐木虱的虫子,会吸食叶片和嫩枝上的汁液,然后分泌出大量白色蜡丝,随风飘扬,落满周围地面,黏黏糊糊。这种虫子非常顽固,难以消灭,所以中国梧桐不是行道树优选。

北山街西湖边，由绿转黄的荷叶和法国梧桐
Yellowing Sycamore Trees and Lotus Leaves at Beishan Street by West Lake

南山路，法国梧桐
Sycamore Trees at Nanshan Road

春季大风天，北山街上梧桐絮飘飞
Wutong Catkins in Spring Air at Beishan Street

中河南路，中国梧桐
Chinese Wutong at Zhonghe South Road

The Wutong Tree:
A Herald of Autumn and
Symbol of Good Fortune

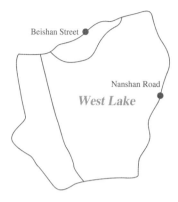

Every year, when it comes to the mid to late November, a classic slogan is about to go online: Autumn in Hangzhou is like a spilled paint tray, colorful and vibrant.

The autumn in Hangzhou is really amazing! Especially on sunny days, the bright sunshine falls on the leaves by the roadside, and the light changes constantly in shadows. Ginkgo biloba, soapberry, maple, Chinese tallow, Canadian maple contribute a picture dotted with a mixture of colors, such as yellow, green, red and orange, which looks particularly beautiful.

But which type of leaf best represents autumn? The Wutong tree comes the first.

The Wutong tree has a close connection with autumn ever since the ancient times. There goes an idiom, "The fall of one leaf is enough to tell the coming of autumn" in "Shuoshanxun" of *Huainanzi* in the Western Han Dynasty. Many people believe that it refers to the leaves of the Wutong tree as it is a big deciduous tree and often starts to wither at the end of summer. Its color change and falling are considered as a sign of autumn.

In the Southern Song Dynasty, the saying of "The Wutong tree is an indication of autumn" became a high-level court ceremony and the tree became an official authoritative "spokesperson for autumn".

In *Records of Mengliang* of the Song Dynasty, there is a vivid description that when the Beginning of Autumn arrived, the imperial official in charge would wear a grand dress with a ceremonial tablet (so-called "hu" in Chinese) in his hand, and rhythmically make the announcement: "Here comes autumn!" At this moment, Wutong leaves would fly down one or two pieces for the occasion in response to the voice of the autumn arrival.

In ancient times, the Wutong tree enjoyed a high social status, not only as a herald of autumn, but also as a symbol of good fortune.

As is said by "The Floods of Autumn" in *Chuang Tzu*: "Starting from the South Sea, the Young Phoenix flies to the Northern Sea; never resting but on the Wutong tree." Wutong trees grow towards the sun and are flourishing. People regard it as a symbol of auspiciousness, which can attract the Phoenix to crow. What kind of Phoenix is in traditional Chinese culture? The legendary auspicious bird is known as the "king of birds". In fact, the Wutong tree can stop the noble Phoenix to have a rest, so its

秋日西湖边北山街的法国梧桐
A Distant View of Sycamores at Beishan Street by West Lake

social status is naturally not inferior.

In many ancient poems, Phoenix and Wutong often made their appearances in pair. As a result, Wutong trees were often planted in the courtyards of former imperial palaces or wealthy families, not only because Wutong trees were tall, upright and imposing, but also because the legend of the Wutong tree attracting the Phoenix was auspicious with favorable implications.

What many people don't know is that Wutong trees, an indicator of autumn, are totally different from those we see on Beishan Street and Nanshan Road today. You may not even have seen the real Wutong tree.

The ancient Wutong tree belongs to the Wutong family, called Chinese Wutong, also called Qingtong ("green Wutong"). It is tall and sturdy, with a straight trunk, green leaves and branches, smooth and green bark, and no nodes.

Strictly speaking, Wutong trees on Beishan Street and Nanshan Road are call "French Wutong", whose real name is Platanus acerifolia (two-ball sycamore), and belongs to the Platanaceae family. They don't pay attention to the "body" management as Chinese Wutong does. The trunk is usually thick and prone to grow crooked. The barks of old trees peel off in patches, revealing greenish white barks after peeling.

The Wutong tree in Hangzhou is not really from France. In the 17th century, in Oxford, England, people used one-ball sycamore (also called American Wutong) and three-ball sycamore (also called French Wutong) as parents to cross into two-ball sycamore, named "English Wutong". After extensive cultivation in Europe, the French brought it to China as a street tree, thus called "French Wutong".

The two-ball sycamore tree grows thick and robust with a long age, and has the largest number among the roadside trees in Hangzhou, accounting for over 40%. It has strong adaptability, fast growth, strong shade in summer, and more sunlight in winter by falling leaves, which makes it the best choice for roadside trees in Hangzhou. According to the incomplete statistics from the Greening Department of Hangzhou Municipal Bureau of Garden and Cultural Relics, there are currently over 42,000 sycamore trees planted in Hangzhou.

Due to its excellent seasonal light transmission effect, the sycamore tree is known as the "king of street trees" according to the principle of "the survival of the fittest", while the popularity of Chinese Wutong is much smaller.

The sycamore tree, favored by many people in China, is nevertheless a great nuisance with its flying catkins in spring.

Ever since 2019, the landscape and greening department has carried out the suppression of Wutong catkins by injecting liquid medicine into the trunk. The spiral administration of medicine through the trunk can help the plants receive medicine more evenly, and also better absorb and decompose drugs, so as to achieve better inhibition effect. Over the past two years, a special batch of low fruiting sycamore trees has been planted, which has few or even no cones. It is a new variety of sycamore tree that does not fly catkins.

At the end of autumn and the beginning of winter, the sycamore trees on Beishan Street and Nanshan Road are likely to look better. When you go outdoors to enjoy autumn, you might as well look for the Chinese Wutong in this city. After all, it is the real "Wutong tree".

So, where else can we find Chinese Wutong in Hangzhou today?

According to the experts from the Greening Department of Hangzhou Municipal Bureau of Garden and Cultural Relics, relatively few Wutong trees have been planted in Hangzhou, many of which were planted in the affiliated green space of the unit around the 1990s, very few in the public green space. A few years ago, a special statistical investigation was made, the result of which shows that there are 259 Chinese Wutong trees in total in the whole city of Hangzhou. The place with the most planted Wutong trees is on Zhonghe South Road with 172 trees, which is also the only road in Hangzhou that uses Chinese Wutong as the street tree. Others are scattered randomly in Zhaohui Community, Laodong Road, Jiangjun Road, Wushan Road, Haichao Road and Xiaozi Lane.

There is also an interesting saying about Chinese Wutong that it can not only predict the coming of autumn, but also feel the presence of the "leap year". It is said that on each branch, it has 12 leaves in normal years with 6 leaves on each side, but 13 leaves in leap years, for which, as it should be, there is no scientific justification. It is just a coincidence, but it gives Chinese Wutong a romantic and poetic connotation.

Then, why wasn't the Chinese Wutong, so valued by the ancients, be widely planted in Hangzhou thereafter?

Of course, there are reasons for this. The main one is that it is quite vulnerable to pests and diseases. There is a kind of insect called green wood louse on the Wutong tree, which has a liking for sucking the juice on the leaves and twigs, and then secretes a large amount of white wax filaments, floating in the wind and falling on the surrounding ground, so sticky for pedestrian's experience. This kind of insect is very difficult to deal with, even harder to kill, so Chinese Wutong fails to become the best choice for street trees.

浴鹄湾
Yuhu Bay

曲院风荷
Breeze-Ruffled Lotus at Quyuan Garden

泛舟湖上，
荡入画中

茅家埠 ●

乌龟潭 ●

浴鹄湾 ●

西湖

春夏交替的杭州，是最适合"走水路"的季节，想要沉浸式感受西湖的绿意盎然，"正确的打开方式"是坐船。

有一条小众的西湖游船线路很火，这条水道主要集中在杨公堤西侧水域，将茅家埠、乌龟潭、浴鹄湾等景点串联，组成了一片"绿野仙踪"。

与热闹的外湖水域不同，这里藏在西湖深处，被称为"西湖秘境中的秘境"，可以解锁观看西湖的新角度。

从岳坟码头出发，船一路往西开，碧波荡漾。穿过第一个拱桥桥洞后，瞬间就切换了"画风"，隔绝了车水马龙的喧嚣，满眼只剩下苍翠欲滴的绿意和偶尔路过的灵动水鸟。不同于外湖的开阔，这里沿途水路曲径通幽，十分静谧。

有人说，再"褶皱"的心情到了这湖上都能被抚平。

美妙的感受从曲院风荷开始。夏日来临时，满园荷花盛开，莲叶田田，映衬着岸旁的亭台轩榭、楼阁拱桥，就是一卷绝美的诗画江南图了。

船继续前行，往西湖更深处去，会经过金沙港水域、杭州花圃；再一路到茅家埠，又会穿过许多个古桥桥洞，有人认真数过，走完整条杨公堤景区游线，一共要穿过 27 个桥洞。

快要过桥洞的时候，记得一定要端起相机，因为这个绝佳机位，只有坐船才能独享。

湖水清澈，半圆拱形的桥洞倒影与水上桥洞合为一体，似一轮满月，这个圆，装满了湖山胜景。尤其是在大晴天的时候，还会有粼粼波光倒映到桥身上。

沿途草木葱绿，好像也不会惦记各色绚烂春花了，光是绿色就可以这么迷人。

过了杭州花圃，就是整个新西湖线路里最为开阔的一片水域——茅家埠，茅乡水情景点。

这里的湖床底层铺植着大片净化水质的水生植物，如亚洲苦草和狐尾草等，它们就像一个个"净水器"一样，确保水环境的安全，也让水面看上去格外清澈。对"居住环境"要求颇高的各类水鸟，也尤为青睐茅家埠，像苍鹭、夜鹭、白鹭等都聚集在此地。

在人迹罕至的茅家埠深处，还有一片鸟儿每天"开例会"的地方。这座迷你的"鹭岛"，居住着数以百计的夜鹭。夜鹭是目前西湖里最大的水鸟家族之一。它们有时站在枝头或湖中央的木桩上，有时在湖上肆意飞翔，这是属于西湖自然野趣的另一面。

再往前，进入西里湖，经过西湖国宾馆附近的水鸟保护区，蜿蜒的水道一直通到乌龟潭、于谦祠，穿过又一个桥洞之后，便来到三台云水景区。

其中的浴鹄湾，也有一个很出片的机位——霁虹桥，它如白色长龙飞卧在水中央。

到这里，整条游线已经接近尾声。缓缓穿过杨公堤自北而南的最后一座桥浚源桥，到花港观鱼码头，再返回岳坟码头。这样一圈行舟时间，大约 1 小时20 分钟。

因为要穿行桥洞，加上航道比较狭窄，西湖里稍大一点的船受到高度限制都进不来，因此能进入杨公堤景区这片水域的只有三种船，除了小型画舫休闲船，还有手划船和摇橹船。

考虑到生态负荷（过多船只活动会影响水鸟、水生植物）、作业保洁、安全救援等因素，目前航线内的手划船、摇橹船和小型画舫休闲船都是限量的。

每条手划（摇橹）船上都有专属的二维码，乘船时，记得扫一扫，可以进入"西湖手划（摇橹）船服务监督评价"系统。确认订单后就可以计时，确保消费透明规范；结束后还可以给船工的服务进行评价打分，也帮助管理部门对整个订单进行全程的后台监管。

手划船每船一般可以乘坐 4—6 人；摇橹船每船是 8—10 人；小型画舫休闲船可以容纳 10—14 人，船内有空调，目前只接待 10—14 人的团队包船。

最后，再给大家"安利"另外一条西湖环湖游览线路。与前面推荐的小众游线相比，环湖游览线路要更加日常一点，一个人就可以乘船；价格也相对实惠，相当于水上公交。尤其是在节假日景区拥堵的时候，这条水路非常推荐。

这条游线一共 10 个站点，各站点票价 6—8 元，如果你想环湖游一圈，全站票价 70 元。线路自亭湾骑射(一公园)出发，中途停靠湖滨晴雨（五公园）、断桥残雪（少年宫）、平湖秋月（中山公园）、花好月圆（杭州饭店）、曲院风荷（郭庄）、茅乡水情（都锦生故居）、花港观鱼、十八相送（长桥）、钱祠表忠（钱王祠），最后回亭湾骑射（一公园）。秘境水域和热门景点都涉及了，一圈下来，差不多 1 小时。

人在船上坐，船在画中游。正值气候宜人的好时节，泛舟西湖可好？

睡莲
Water Lilies

水鸟
A Waterbird

131

浴鹄湾，泛舟赏景
Boat Tour on Yuhu Bay

杨公堤环璧桥
Huanbi Bridge on Yanggong Causeway

Boating on the Lake: Drifting into a Living Painting

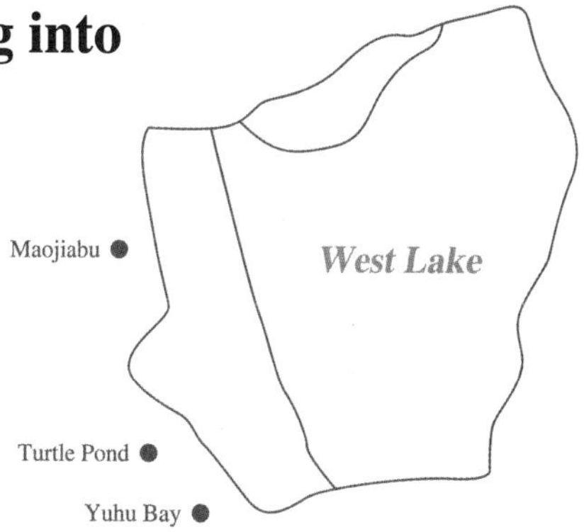

Maojiabu ●

West Lake

Turtle Pond ●

Yuhu Bay ●

In Hangzhou, the time between spring and summer is the most favorable season for "sightseeing by water". If you want to immerse yourself in the lush greenery of West Lake, it is better to spend your journey by boat.

There is a niche West Lake cruise route that is very popular and mainly around the waters west of Yanggong Causeway. It is connected one by one by attractions such as Maojiabu, Turtle Pond, and Yuhu Bay, thus staging "the Wizard of Oz".

Different from the bustling waters of the outer lake, this place is hidden deep in West Lake and is known as the "secret realm of West Lake", which can create new perspectives for viewing West Lake.

Departing from Yue Fei's Tomb Pier, the boat sails westward with rippling blue waves. After passing through the first arch bridge opening, there comes an instant change in scenery: without any hustle and bustle of the traffic, and all that could be seen are the lush greenery and occasionally lively waterbirds passing by. Unlike the open waters of the outer lake, the waterways throughout the journey are winding and peaceful.

It is said that even the most wrinkled emotions can be smoothed out on this lake.

The fantastic feeling begins from the scenic spot "Breeze-ruffled Lotus at Quyuan Garden". When summer comes, the garden is filled with blooming lotus flowers and fields of lotus leaves, reflecting the pavilions and arch bridges by the shore, thus a beautiful picture of Jiangnan with poetic images will come into the view.

The boat continues to move deeper into West Lake, passing through the waters of Jinsha Port, Hangzhou Flower Nursery, and then to Maojiabu. Meanwhile, it also sails through many ancient bridge openings during the journey. It has been carefully counted that the tour route of entire Yanggong Causeway Scenic Area has 27 bridge openings in total.

When you are about to pass through bridge openings, keep in mind to pick up your camera as this excellent shooting position can only be enjoyed by taking a boat.

At a glance, bridge openings in the shape of semi-circular arch are integrated with their reflections in the clear lake water like a full moon, which is filled with beautiful scenery of the lake and mountains nearby. Especially on sunny days, there are sparkling waves reflecting on bridges.

Along the way, the vegetation is lush and green, which makes the tourists forget the colorful spring flowers. Just the greenery can be so charming and beautiful.

After passing by Hangzhou Flower Nursery, here comes the most open water area in the entire new West Lake route — represented by the scenic spots such as Maojiabu and Water Scenery at Maoxiang.

In general, the bottom layer of the lake is covered with large areas of aquatic plants that can purify water quality, such as Asian bitters and foxtail grass, they act like "water purifiers" to ensure the safety of the water environment. Thus, the water surface looks particularly clear. In addition, various waterbirds with high requirements for living environment also show their special preference to Maojiabu, where herons, night herons, egrets, and others gather.

In the depths of rarely-visited Maojiabu, there is a small "Egret Island" where birds hold daily meetings. It is home to hundreds of night herons, which are currently one of the largest water bird families in West Lake. They sometimes stand on the branches or wooden stakes in the center of the lake, and sometimes fly freely on the lake, which is another side of the natural wildness of West Lake.

Further ahead is Xili Lake. The winding waterway along the waterbird conservation area near Xihu State Guesthouse leads all the way to Turtle Pond and Yuqian Temple. After passing through another bridge opening, you are supposed to arrive at the scenic area of Clouds Floating on the Water Surface on Santai Mountain.

In this area, there is Yuhu Bay, which also has a very impressive scenic spot called Jihong Bridge, like a white dragon flying in the middle of the water.

At this point, the entire tour comes to its end. The following route goes in sequence as follows: Junyuan Bridge (the last bridge of Yanggong Causeway from north to south), Viewing Fish at the Flower Harbor Pier, and then a return to Yue Fei's Tomb Pier. This round of cruise takes about 1 hour and 20 minutes.

Due to the need to voyage through bridge openings and narrow waterways, larger boats in West Lake are limited in height and cannot make their access. Therefore, there are only three types of boats that can enter the Yanggong Causeway scenic area. In addition to small painted leisure boats, there are also hand-rowed boats and rowing boats.

Considering the ecological load (excessive boat activities can affect waterbirds and aquatic plants), operational cleaning, safety rescue, etc., currently the number of hand-rowed boats, rowing boats, and small painted leisure boats on the route is under control.

Each hand-rowed (rowing) boat has an exclusive QR code. When boarding, remember to scan it to enter the "West Lake Hand-rowed Boat Service Supervision and Evaluation" system. After the order confirmation, it can be timed to ensure transparent and standardized consumption. At the end of the journey, the service of the boatman can be evaluated and scored, which helps the management department in the background to supervise the entire process of the order.

The hand-rowed boats can generally accommodate 4−6 tourists per boat; while the rowing boat 8−10 tourists per boat and the small painted leisure boat 10−14 tourists per boat with air conditioning inside. Currently, the small painted leisure boat only accepts package group of 10−14 tourists.

Finally, another tour route around West Lake is to be introduced for reference. Compared with the previously recommended niche tour route, the lake tour route is more daily. You can take a boat, and the price is relatively affordable, similar to a water bus. Especially during holidays when scenic spots are congested, this waterway is highly recommended.

There are 10 stops in total, with ticket prices ranging from 6−8 *yuan* per stop. If you want to take a loop tour around the lake, the total ticket price is 70 *yuan*. The route departs from Horseback Archery at Tingwan (The 1st Park), stopping midway at Sunny and Rainy Views from the Lakeside (The 5th Park), Melting Snow on the Broken Bridge (Children's Palace), Autumn Moon on the Calm Lake (Zhongshan Park), Blooming Flowers and Full Moon (Pier of Shangri-La Hangzhou), Breeze-ruffled Lotus at Quyuan Garden (Guozhuang), Water Scenery at Maoxiang (Former Residence of Du Jinsheng), Viewing Fish at the Flower Harbor, Eighteen Send-offs (Long Bridge), Praise of King Qian's Loyalty in His Shrine (Temple of King Qian), and finally returning to Horseback Archery at Tingwan (The 1st Park). The secret waters and popular attractions are both involved, and it takes about an hour to circle around.

This scene of sitting on the boat which drifts in the picture is likely to leave you the question: is it good to go boating on West Lake during the pleasant climate and good season?

天气晴热，坐船透过桥洞望去，西湖风景如画
A Picturesque View of West Lake from a Boat through a Bridge Opening on a Hot Day

花港观鱼
Viewing Fish at Flower Pond

浴鹄湾霁虹桥
Jihong Bridge at Yuhu Bay

西湖秘境
West Lake Wonderland

穗庐通往北山街的石阶
Suilu Cottage's Stone Steps Leading to Beishan Street

北山街上被遗忘的百年宅邸

穗庐

西湖

在杭州，你可能很难再找到一条像北山街这样地理位置绝佳的道路。

它坐北朝南，依山面水，风光无限。

从清末开始，这里便成为达官显贵追逐的安家之处。一拨又一拨军政要员、社会名流、富商巨贾把目光投向这里，在西子湖畔打造自己的人生传奇。

在众多有故事的民国别墅、名庐中间，有一处已荒废多年的穗庐，始终低调而隐秘。

穗庐里有一个观景露台，这两年在社交网站上突然走红，因为在这里，你可以眺望曲院风荷、玉带桥与雷峰塔。不少人专程赶来打卡，只为能拍到一张山、水、湖、塔同框的绝美大片。

很多人好奇，穗庐到底在哪个位置？它曾经的主人是谁，又有多少不平凡的过往？

北山街94号，这是穗庐的门牌号。但说实话，从北山街走过无数遍的人，可能也从来没发现过它的存在。

一个重要的原因是，穗庐不在路边，且石阶的直通大门紧闭。找到它，需要绕道爬山。

杨公堤与北山街交叉口有一条登山游步道，走一小段，能看到右手边有一排老房子，从这里便可以通往穗庐。

一条长长的石阶，直达北山街，走下去就能看到一座雕刻精美的砖饰门楼，门楣居中位置写着"穗庐"二字。

穗，是广东广州的别称，言简意赅，这是广州人建的房子。门口的石碑介绍说，入口牌坊由清水砖砌成，颇具岭南建筑风格。

这是一座保存较完整的集住宅、祠堂、家坟于一体的山地园林式花园别墅。院内是两层三开间的老式洋房，具有浓郁的民国风情，中西合璧。

穗庐又名鲍庄，始建于民国11年（1922），民国14年（1925）建成，已经有近百年历史。它的主人是广东富商鲍柏麟，曾在广州、上海、杭州等地经营多种产业，家底殷实。

再上石阶，走到高处，回头俯瞰，整个建筑掩映在300多岁的古樟树中间，墙面沧桑斑驳，院内落叶满地。时间在这里好像是静止的，孤寂、萧索又绵长。

在这北山街上，名人故居实在太多，从民国时期浙江省政府主席张静江的"静逸别墅"，到报业巨子史量才和爱妻沈秋水的"秋水山庄"，再到北山街8号的蒋经国故居等。相比之下，已荒废多年的穗庐，难免就显得寂寞一点。

只有继续沿着石阶，走到半山观景露台处，才有了人气。

许多慕名而来的年轻游客和摄影爱好者，在这个背山面湖的取景点眺望西湖，打卡社交平台上的爆款拍照点位。

露台上，有一座混凝土结构的八角雕花亭，采用了中国传统建筑形式，体现了中西合璧的时代特点。坐在亭中，远眺西湖，算得上是一处绝佳秘境。

除了网红摄影打卡地，很多人不知道，这里也曾是文人聚集的地方。

2004年，穗庐被列入杭州市第一批历史建筑。一年之后，"江南文学会馆"搬到这里，不少当代文坛大佬都曾到过这里，书香在这里弥漫开来，直到后来文学会馆迁出，才空置至今。

与穗庐一墙之隔的北山街95号建筑，也曾是江南文学会馆的办公区域。这里原为著名士绅汪曼锋于1934年所建的私宅。汪曼锋与浙江著名人物陈叔通、马寅初私交深厚。

除了八角石亭，还有一座四角石方亭，就在穗庐后院的石阶旁。亭子周围藤蔓密布，很容易就错过了。但必须提一提，不少文学爱好者知道穗庐，就是因为这座亭子。因为亭子中央有一座水泥方碑，上面有巴金先生的手模。

石碑侧面，还刻着巴金手迹"我的心灵中燃烧着希望之火"和"讲真话，把心交给读者"；正面则刻着戏剧大师曹禺称赞巴金的话——"你是光，你是热，你是二十世纪的良心"。

巴金对西湖一往情深，曾在《随想录》中写道："全国也有不少令人难忘的名胜古迹，我却偏爱西湖。我十岁前就知道一些关于西湖的事情，岳王坟占着最高的地位。以后我每次来西湖，都要到这座坟前徘徊一阵……岳飞、牛皋、于谦、张煌言、秋瑾……我看到的不是坟，他们是不灭的存在，是崇高理想和献身精神的化身。西湖是和这样的人、这样的精神结合在一起的，它不仅美丽，而且光辉。"

距离穗庐不远处就是岳王庙，这可能也是当年巴金喜欢这片庄园的原因之一。

亭子里这个手模，是由北京现代文学馆制作、巴金女儿李小林赠送给杭州的。而这个亭子，也被取名为"巴金亭"。

浙江省作家协会副主席王旭烽曾评价穗庐："西湖的文气，江南的诗意，中华民族的神韵，尽可在这里寻觅。"

四角石方亭（巴金亭）
Ba Jin Pavilion (Four-Cornered Square Stone Pavilion)

巴金手迹"江南文学会馆"石碑
The Stele with Ba Jin's Handwritten "Jiangnan Literature Association" Inscription

八角石亭
The Octagonal Stone Pavilion

The Forgotten Century-Old Mansion on Beishan Street

In Hangzhou, it may be difficult to find another road with an excellent geographical location like Beishan Street.

Facing north and south, with mountains and water, the scenery in Beishan Street is infinite.

Since the end of the Qing Dynasty, this place has become a popular destination for high-ranking officials and nobles. Waves of military and political officials, social celebrities, and wealthy businessmen have cast their eyes on this place, creating their own life legends by West Lake.

Among the villas and famous houses of the Republic of China with many stories, there is a long-abandoned Suilu Cottage that has always been low-keyed and secretive.

Right in Suilu Cottage, there is a viewing terrace which has suddenly become popular on social media in the past two years because here, you can overlook the Jade Belt Bridge of Breeze-ruffled Lotus at Quyuan Garden and Leifeng Pagoda. Many people arrive here specifically to update the moment, just to capture a stunning picture of mountains, waters, lakes, and towers in the same frame.

Many people are curious about: where Suilu Cottage is located? who was its former owner and how many extraordinary experiences has it had?

No. 94 Beishan Street, this is the house number of Suilu Cottage. But to be honest, even people who have walked through Beishan Street many times may never have noticed its existence.

One important reason is that Suilu Cottage is not on the roadside and the stone steps leading directly to it are tightly closed. To find it, you need to take a detour and climb the mountain.

At the intersection of Yanggong Causeway and Beishan Street, there is a hiking trail. After walking a short distance, you can see a row of old houses on your right, which leads to Suilu Cottage.

A long stone staircase leads directly to Beishan Street, and as you walk down, you will see a elegantly-carved brick archway with the inscription of two Chinese characters "Sui Lu" in the center of the lintel.

"Sui" is another name for Guangzhou of Guangdong. Simply put, this is the house of Guangzhou people. According to the introduction stone tablet in the doorway, the entrance memorial archway is made of clear water brick, which features Lingnan architectural style.

This is a well-preserved villa with mountain garden style that integrates residential buildings, ancestral halls, and family graves. Inside the courtyard is an old-fashioned two-story house in western style, which is three times of the standard width of a room. Moreover, it is characterized by an integration of Chinese and Western elements with a strong Republican style.

Suilu Cottage, also known as Baozhuang, was founded in 1922 and completed in 1925, with a history of nearly a hundred years. Its owner was Bao Bailin, a wealthy businessman from Guangdong who had run various industries in Guangzhou, Shanghai, Hangzhou and other places, and had a well-off family background.

After you climb up the stone steps to reach a high place and look back, the entire building is nestled among ancient camphor trees that are over 300 years old. The walls are weathered and mottled, and the courtyard is covered in fallen leaves. Time seems to be static here, lonely, desolate, and lingering.

On Beishan Street, there are too many old residences of the celebrity, from the "Jingyi Villa" of Zhejiang Provincial Government Chairman Zhang Jingjiang from the Republic of China Period, to the "Qiushui Villa" of newspaper tycoon Shi Liangcai and his beloved wife Shen Qiushui, to the old residence of Chiang Chingkuo at No. 8 Beishan Street, and so on. In contrast, the abandoned Suilu Cottage for many years inevitably appears a bit lonely.

Only by continuous climbing along the stone steps and reaching the observation terrace halfway up the mountain, does one discover a little bit of popularity.

Young tourists and photography enthusiasts who are attracted to come here by its reputation visit this scenic spot with mountains and lakes on its back, and update the moment of West Lake at the popular photo spots on social media platforms.

On the terrace, there is an octagonal carved pavilion with a concrete structure, which adopts traditional Chinese architectural forms and embodies the characteristics of the integration of Chinese and Western styles. Sitting in the pavilion to overlook West Lake, it can be considered as an excellent place with a hint of mystery.

Apart from being a popular photo spot for internet celebrities, many people are unaware that this place used to be a gathering place for literati.

In 2004, Suilu Cottage was listed in the first batch of historical buildings in Hangzhou. One year later, Jiangnan Literature Association made its settlement here. Many contemporary literary giants had once been here, which endowed the place with dense academic atmosphere. It was not until Jiangnan Literature Association moved out that it remained vacant until now.

The building at No. 95 Beishan Street, separated by a wall from Suilu Cottage, was also the office area of Jiangnan Literature Association. It was originally a private residence built by the famous gentry Wang Manfeng in 1934, who had deep personal relationships with famous Zhejiang figures Chen Shutong and Ma Yinchu.

In addition to the octagonal stone pavilion, there is also a square stone pavilion with four corners, located next to the stone steps in the backyard of Suilu Cottage. The pavilion is hidden in the dense vines and is easy to get ignored. But it should be noted that many literary enthusiasts know about Suilu Cottage because of this pavilion, in which there is a cement square monument in the center, with Mr. Ba Jin's fingerprints on it.

On the side of the stone tablet, there are also inscriptions by Ba Jin: "The flame of hope burns in my heart" and "Tell the truth and hand over my heart to the reader". On the front are engraved the words of drama master Cao Yu praising Ba Jin—You are the light, you are the heat, you are the conscience of the 20th century.

Ba Jin has a deep affection for West Lake and once wrote in *Random Thoughts*: "There are also many unforgettable scenic spots and historical sites throughout the country, but I prefer West Lake. I knew something about West Lake before I was ten years old, and Yue Fei's Tomb held the highest position. Afterwards, every time I came to West Lake, I would wander around this tomb for a while... Yue Fei, Niu Gao, Yu Qian, Zhang Huangyan, Qiu Jin... What I saw is not graves, they are immortal beings, embodiments of lofty ideals and dedication. West Lake is deeply integrated with such people and such spirit, which is not only beautiful, but also radiant."

Not far from Suilu Cottage is Yue Fei's Temple, which may have been one of the reasons why Ba Jin gave his preference to this place.

The fingerprints in the pavilion were made by Beijing Museum of Modern Literature and gifted to Hangzhou by Li Xiaolin, the daughter of Ba Jin. And this pavilion is also named "Ba Jin Pavilion".

As Wang Xufeng, Vice Chairman of Zhejiang Provincial Writers Association, once commented on Suilu Cottage, "The literary charm of West Lake, the poctic charm of Jiangnan, and the spirit of the Chinesc nation can all be found here."

西湖小南湖入水口，一条条白鲢跃出水面，翻入闸口，上演"鱼跃龙门""西湖飞鱼"的奇特景象，不少市民和游客驻足围观
At the Inlet of Xiaonan Lake in West Lake, White Silver Carps Leap into the Sluice Gate, Creating Spectacular Scenes of "Fish Leaping over the Dragon Gate" and "Flying Fish of West Lake", Which Have Attracted Many Residents and Tourists

西湖"鱼口普查"

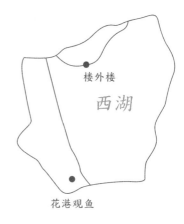

西湖从哪里来？

古时候的杭州是一片汪洋大海，西湖所在的位置为一处浅海海湾。随着海平面下降和钱塘江潮挟带泥沙大量淤积，在距今约 2000 年前，隔出了一片湖，这就是西湖最初的样子。

后来，周围山区多条溪流把淡水和泥沙带入，西湖不断淡化成了淡水湖。

这么大一片西湖，少不了请鱼儿们来当常住民，甚至很长一段时间，西湖就是专门用来养鱼的。

据史料记载，西湖鱼类养殖始于唐代。长庆四年（824），白居易在《钱塘湖石记》提到湖水灌溉要重于鱼龙菱芡的养殖。

到 1949 年，杭州专门成立了西湖养鱼社；1951 年，西湖养鱼社又更名西湖水产养殖场；后几经更名，到 1981 年，养殖场才正式改为西湖水域管理处，工作重心也发生变化，以管理为主，养鱼为辅，更加关注西湖水质的保护。

当时，随着杭州城市的发展，各种污染因素也在增加，造成西湖水质恶化。根据水域管理处工作人员回忆，1981 年西湖水体透明度只有 17 至 18 厘米，"水是蓝黑色的，最严重时用白瓷碗舀起来，碗都会变黑"。坊间也在质疑，在西湖里养鱼会造成水质污染吗？

1983年10月，水域管理处牵头组织了一次全国性的学术讨论会，有环保、水产、园林方面全国顶尖的专家参加。与会的五六十位专家讨论后，一致认为合理养鱼是不会污染水质的。于是，西湖养鱼的传统，一直延续至今。

鱼类是水生态系统中的重要组成部分，在维持食物网结构与功能中发挥重要作用。湖泊鱼类群落结构特征将直接决定湖泊生态系统的结构与功能。

今天的西湖水环境是肉眼可见的好，湖水碧于染，锦鳞活水鱼，绕岸众莺啼。水质清澈，鱼的种类也越来越丰富。

这些鱼类主要以藻类等浮游生物为"主食"，可以有效遏制藻类大量生长，对净化水质、保持湖水透明度有重要作用。

2022年5月15日，新华社刊发《西湖首次鱼类调查发现36种鱼栖居》一文，研究发现，当时西湖中生活着36种鱼。

这项2021年至2022年由西湖水域管理处进行的调查显示，这36种鱼隶属于5目9科28属，以鲤科鱼类为主。似鳔（jiǎo）、鲫、鲹（cān）、黄尾密鲴（gù）和鳙（yōng）是杭州西湖的优势鱼类。

目前在西湖"长期定居"的鱼类主要有以下这些：

白鲢，被称为"水中清道夫"。白鲢幼鱼能主动游入河湾或湖泊中索饵，以浮游植物为主食，但是鱼苗阶段仍以浮游动物为食，是一种典型的浮游生物食性的鱼类。

花鲢，学名鳙鱼，杭州人更愿意叫它包头鱼。它和鲤鱼一个科，鲤科鳙属。

草鱼，和青鱼、鲢、鳙并称我国淡水养殖的"四大家鱼"。

鲤鱼，平时多栖息于江河、湖泊、水库、池沼的水草丛生的水体底层，以底栖动物为主食，适应性强，耐寒、耐碱、耐缺氧。鲤鱼是品种最多、分布最广、养殖历史最悠久、产量最高的淡水鱼类之一。

黄尾密鲴，俗名黄尾、黄片等，是一种中小型经济鱼类，生活在水体的中下层，以附生硅藻、水底腐殖质和高等水生植物的碎屑为食。

鲫鱼，主要生活在西湖底层水域中。它的"同楼层邻居"还包括黄颡（sǎng）鱼、南方大口鲇、鲤鱼、青鱼、泥鳅、乌鳢、鳜鱼、黄鳝等；住在"鲫鱼"楼上的西湖中下层水域的鱼类，则有草鱼、高体鳑鲏（páng pí）、华鳈（quán）、团头鲂、中华鳑鲏等；西湖最上层水域"景观房"居住的鱼类主要包括鳌鲦、红鳍原鲌（bó）、鲢鱼、翘嘴鲌、鳙鱼等。

鳊鱼，一听到这个名字，是不是就想到了葱油鳊鱼？鳊鱼为草食性鱼类，食性范围较广，以苦草、轮叶黑藻、眼子菜等水生维管束植物为主要食料，也喜欢吃陆生禾本科植物和菜叶，还能摄食部分湖底植物碎屑和少量浮游动物。

黄颡鱼，也就是杭州人很熟悉的汪刺鱼。黄颡鱼多栖息于缓流多水草的湖周浅水区和入湖河流处，营底栖生活，尤其喜欢生活在静水或缓流的浅滩处、腐殖质多和淤泥多的地方。

看到这里，或许有吃货朋友们会关心，哪里才能买到正宗的西湖鱼？就在东山弄农贸市场里。很多老杭州都知道这里的西湖鱼亭，卖的是野生的西湖鱼，没有泥土腥气。

赶早的市民一般都会拿着水桶直接来买鱼，每天都有新鲜的西湖鱼从茅家埠鱼码头运到菜市场里，营业时间从早上 6 点半到下午 5 点半，售完为止。

跟卖西湖莲蓬一样，卖西湖鱼也要有捕捞权才能抓来卖，全杭州仅此一处能买到西湖活鱼。

市民吃野生鱼，都是跟着季节吃：春天吃步鱼，夏天有西湖黄，冬天吃包头鱼。每天抓到什么就卖什么，一年四季都是鲜的。

西湖水暖，一条鲤鱼追逐野鸭，溅起水花

In the Warm Waters of West Lake, a Carp Chases a Wild Duck, Creating Crisp Splashes

西湖北里湖，水清鱼乐
Fish Swimming Joyfully in the Clear Waters of Beili Lake, West Lake

"Fish Population Census" of West Lake

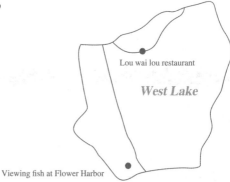

Lou wai lou restaurant

West Lake

Viewing fish at Flower Harbor

Where does West Lake come from?

In ancient times, Hangzhou was a vast ocean, and the location of West Lake was a shallow sea bay. With the decline of sea level and the accumulation of sediments carried by the Qiantang River tide, a lake came to its formation about 2,000 years ago, which was the initial shape of West Lake.

Later on, multiple streams in the surrounding mountainous areas brought in fresh water and sediments, and West Lake gradually desalinated into a freshwater lake.

For such a large lake, it is inevitable to invite fish to become permanent residents. In fact, West Lake has been specifically used for fish farming for a long period of time.

According to the historical records, fish farming in West Lake began in the Tang Dynasty. In the fourth year of Changqing (824 AD), Bai Juyi mentioned in his article "Stone Records of Qiantang Lake" that lake water irrigation should be more important than the cultivation of fish and water chestnut.

Hangzhou established the West Lake Fish Farming Society in 1949, and two years later, it was renamed West Lake Aquaculture Farm. After several changes, its name was officially determined as the West Lake Water Management Office in 1981 with its work focus changed into management, supplemented by fish farming. Moreover, more attention has been paid to the protection of West Lake water quality.

At that time, with the development of Hangzhou city, various pollution factors were also increasing, resulting in the deterioration of water quality in West Lake. According to the recollection of the staff in the Water Management Office, the transparency of West Lake water was only 17 to 18 centimeters in 1981. "The water was bluish black, and at its worst, when scooped up with a white porcelain bowl, the bowl would turn black." As a result, it was questioned by the public whether raising fish in West Lake would bring about water pollution?

In October 1983, the Water Management Office led a national academic symposium with top experts in environmental protection, aquaculture, and landscaping. After 50−60 experts' discussion, it was unanimously agreed that reasonable fish farming would not pollute water quality. So, the tradition of raising fish in West Lake has continued to this day.

As a component of aquatic ecosystems, the fish plays a crucial role in maintaining the structure and function of the food chain. The structural characteristics of fish communities in lakes will directly determine the structure and function of lake ecosystems.

The water environment of West Lake today is incredibly good, visible to all, with the lake water being bluer than the blue dye, fish swimming merrily in the water, and warblers singing around the shore. Thanks to the excellent water quality, the variety of fish is becoming increasingly abundant.

These fish mainly feed on planktonic organisms such as algae, which can effectively curb the massive growth of algae and play an important role in purifying water quality and maintaining the transparency of lake water.

On May 15, 2022, Xinhua News Agency delivered an article entitled "The First Fish Survey in West Lake Discovers 36 Fish Species", which indicates that there are currently 36 fish species living in West Lake.

The survey conducted by the West Lake Water Management Office from 2021 to 2022 shows that 36 fish species belong to 5 orders, 9 families, and 28 genera, with cyprinidae fish being the main species. Toxabramis swinhonis, crucian carp, hemicculter leuciclus, yellow tailed catfish, and bighead carp are dominant fish species in West Lake of Hangzhou.

The main fish species that have long settled in West Lake are as follows.

Silver carp. It is known as a water cleaner, and juvenile silver carp can actively swim into river bays or lakes to feed on planktonic plants as their main food. However, during the fry stage, they still feed on planktonic animals, making them a typical planktonic feeding fish.

Variegated carp. The scientific name is bighead carp, and Hangzhou people prefer to call it "Baotou fish". It belongs to the same family as carp, the carp family.

Grass carp. Together with black carp, silver carp and variegated carp, they are called China's "four famous domestic fishes" of the freshwater aquaculture.

Carp. The carp usually lives in the bottom layer of the water body with aquatic plants growing in rivers, lakes, reservoirs, and ponds. It is mainly benthic animal with strong adaptability, cold resistance, alkali resistance, and hypoxia resistance. The carp is one of the freshwater fish species with the largest variety, widest distribution, longest breeding history, and highest yield.

Yellow tailed catfish. Commonly known as Huangwei, Huangpian, etc., it is a small and medium-sized economic fish that lives in the middle and lower layers of water bodies, feeding on attached diatoms, bottom humus, and debris from higher aquatic plants.

Crucian carp. Everyone is familiar with crucian carp. As for its place of residence, the crucian carp in West Lake mainly lives in the bottom layer of water. Its neighbors on the same layer include yellow catfish, southern catfish, carp, black carp, loach, black snakehead, mandarin fish, yellow eel, etc. Besides, the fish living in the middle and lower water bodies of West Lake above the crucian carp include grass carp, high bodied bream, Chinese bream, round headed bream, rhodeus sinensis, etc. The fish species living on the top layer of West Lake, accessible to views, mainly include hemicculter leuciclus, red finned original culter, silver carp, culter alburnus, bighead carp, etc.

White bream. Does this name immediately bring "scallion oil" to your mind? The white bream is an herbivorous fish with a wide range of feeding habits. It mainly feeds on aquatic vascular plants such as bitter grass, black algae, and eye vegetables. It also likes to eat terrestrial grasses and vegetable leaves, as well as some plant debris and a small number of planktonic animals at the bottom of the lake.

Yellow catfish. Very familiar to locals in Hangzhou, it is also called Wangci fish, which mostly inhabits the shallow waters around the lake with slow flowing water and abundant aquatic plants, as well as the rivers that enter the lake. They live in the bottom, especially dwelling in still water or shallow waters with slow flows, and in places with abundant humus and muds.

Upon this, some foodie friends may be concerned about where to buy authentic West Lake fish? It's in the Dongshan Lane Farmers' Market. Many old Hangzhou natives know about the West Lake Fish Pavilion, where wild West Lake fish with no earthy smell are available.

Early in the morning, residents in Hangzhou usually come directly with buckets to buy fish. Fresh West Lake fish are transported from Maojiabu Fish Pier to the market every day, and the business hours are from 6:30 a.m. to 5:30 p.m. until sold out.

Like lotus seedpods in West Lake, selling West Lake fish also requires fishing rights to catch and sell. Only in this spot in Hangzhou can live West Lake fish be bought.

Wild fish are consumed by residents according to the season. In spring, Bu fish is to be eaten; while in summer and winter, Xihuhuang fish and Baotou fish are served respectively. It is a long-practiced habit to sell whatever fish are caught every day, thus fresh all year round.

水乐洞
Shuiyue Cave

西湖群山深处，
冷门纳凉洞

西湖

水乐洞 ●

　　从满觉陇顺翁家山而上，有三个相距不远的洞穴——石屋洞、水乐洞和烟霞洞，并称"烟霞三洞"，是西湖边最古老的洞壑之一。

　　烟霞洞名声最响，洞里的十八罗汉石刻造像非常有名；如果是晴天去，光线好，还能看到洞内的钟乳石与石笋闪烁五色异彩，宛如烟霞。

　　杭州人对石屋洞也不陌生，它的位置就在满陇桂雨的入口处附近，庭院内遍植桂花，每年秋天，满园子都是香喷喷的，因此这里也成了杭城赏桂的胜地。

　　三洞中，唯有水乐洞略显低调，很多人都没去过。实际上，历史上的它，也曾有过高光时刻——包括苏东坡在内的历代文人墨客，都曾争相到这里游赏，并情不自禁要为它写诗作文。如果宋代有社交平台，水乐洞一定能登上热门打卡景点的榜单。尤其是"上蒸下煮"的三伏天，走进这个纯天然的宝藏避暑山洞，一阵清凉扑面而来，比吹空调还要凉快。

　　水乐洞在南高峰西，烟霞岭下。

　　洞前是一个用石砖围起来的幽静小院子，树木浓荫，门头横额上写着"水乐洞"三字。

　　沿着石径走到洞前，入口处还有一个方形的泉池，里面有小鱼嬉戏，跨过池上的石梁走进洞内，眼前豁然开朗。整个洞全长约 60 米，一共有两处入口，中间以天然巨岩相隔。

人在洞中，可以听到泉水流淌的声音。旁边还摆有石桌和石凳，就放在最适合听这清冷泉韵的位置，供游人歇脚听泉。据说，如果遇上下雨天，这首天然无弦琴演奏的旋律会更加激昂动人。

这可能是杭州最有乐感的洞壑，到底是谁最早为它取的名？这个人叫郑獬（xiè），是北宋的"超级学霸"，他 31 岁时参加廷试，一举高中，取得进士一甲一名的成绩，被宋仁宗钦定为"忠孝状元"。走上仕途后，郑獬一直为官清廉、刚正不阿。北宋熙宁二年（1069），他因反对王安石变法，从开封知府被贬到杭州任知州，心中郁闷的他跟友人来这里游玩，面对"洞中有水，声如金石"的奇景有感而发，于是为其命名"水乐洞"。关于命名这件事，郑獬的好朋友汪辅之记录了下来，就刻在洞内。

郑獬调离杭州，去青州（今山东省青州市）任职的一年之后，杭州百姓迎来了又一位学霸"市长"——苏东坡。

北宋熙宁四年（1071），苏轼刚到杭州任职，就到满觉陇游玩，其中一个"打卡点"就是水乐洞。兴致盎然的他，写下一篇《水乐洞小记》："钱塘东南有水乐洞，泉流岩中，皆自然宫商。"因为天然的石灰岩能起到很好的扩音作用，近千年前，这里的泉水就是"宫商"韵律。

这样看来，现在大家习惯把"水乐洞"的"乐"读成快乐的"乐"（lè），其实正确念法应该是音乐的"乐"（yuè）。为了能听到这奇妙"水乐"，被苏轼"安利"来观瞻探胜的文人还有许多。写《浮生六记》的沈复、近代著名文学家林纾，还有西泠八家之一的黄易等人，纷纷来此打卡题咏。

明代养生专家高濂，十分善于挖掘小众景点，他专门把"水乐洞雨后听泉"列入了自己的养生宝典《遵生八笺》"高子秋时幽赏"里。

文人墨客在泉池周围的岩壁上"跟帖"留言，写得密密麻麻，但由于时间久远，这些刻字大多已被岁月侵蚀，现在能见到的基本是清末至民国的，如"天然琴声""听无弦琴""高山流水""清乐梵音"等。

民国 11 年（1922），国画大师张大千的哥哥、以画虎闻名的张善孖（zī）

携兄弟来水乐洞游玩，留下题刻："汉安张虎痴及其弟丽诚、文修、大千、君绥五人来游于此。"几年之后，书画鉴藏名家吴湖帆也携情人施畹秋游水乐洞，后作诗咏之："空留别院玲珑，一湾流水，听沧海、明珠溅雨。"

除了能听泉水叮咚，历史上的水乐洞还有过许多不同的身份标签。最早的一个，也就是它的前身，是五代吴越王钱弘佐所建的西关净化禅院。在水乐洞边的山石上，刻有《新建镇国资延禅院石像之记》，记录了西关净化禅院的来历，描述它是"立善作福，皆为方便之门；举首低头，尽是可归之路"。

南宋淳熙六年（1179），宋孝宗将这里赏赐给了自己的内侍李隶，重建佛寺，增广园池。到了宋宁宗年间（1195—1224），寺院荒废，水乐洞成了杨郡王的私家园林。杨郡王是山西原平人杨沂中，出身名门，是"杨家将"后人、南宋大将，立下过赫赫战功，曾是岳飞并肩作战的兄弟。就是他，将水乐洞打造成了当时的热门景点。杨沂中也有一段"黑历史"，就是他奉秦桧之命去庐山诱捕岳飞，并被安排监斩岳飞。

周密在《武林旧事》中提到，水乐洞"慈明殿赐杨郡王，后归贾平章。山石奇秀，中一洞嵌空有声，以此得名"。当时的水乐洞作为杨沂中的私人园林，垒石筑亭，结构精雅。后来，这里日久淤塞，逐渐荒芜。南宋丞相贾似道对这里也很感兴趣，便花重金买下，重新修葺了一番，水乐洞得以恢复原貌。

水乐洞在南宋时期几易其主，兴而废、废复兴的这段历史，被明末"西湖深度游第一人"张岱写进了他的《西湖梦寻·烟霞石屋》里。

摩崖石刻
A Cliffside Inscription

留云谷和云门
Liuyun Valley (Cloud Resting Valley) and Yunmen Gate (Cloud Gate)

水乐洞，摩崖石刻
Cliff Inscriptions in Shuiyue Cave

张大千等五人同游摩崖石刻
The Inscription by Zhang Daqian Recording His Visit with Four Friends to Shuiyue Cave

水乐洞
Shuiyue Cave

Hidden Gem:
Cooling Cave in
West Lake's Mountains

West Lake

●
Shuiyue Cave

Upward from Manjuelong along Wengjia Mountain, there are three caves not far apart — Stone House Cave, Shuiyue Cave and Rosy Cloud Cave, collectively known as "Three Rosy Cloud Caves", which are one of the oldest caves by West Lake.

The most renowned Rosy Cloud Cave is famous for its 18 Arhat stone carvings. On sunny days with strong light, it is easy for you to see the stalactites and stalagmites in the cave glittering in different colors, just like the haze.

In fact, people in Hangzhou are quite familiar with the Stone House Cave, which is located near the entrance of the scenic spot of Sweet Osmanthus Rain at Manjuelong Village. Osmanthus flowers are planted throughout the courtyard, and every autumn, the whole garden is sweet-smelling, making it a popular destination for appreciating osmanthus in Hangzhou.

Among the three caves, the Shuiyue Cave is slightly keeping a low profile, and many people have never been there. However, in history, it had a shining moment — Su Dongpo and other literati and poets of all dynastie eagerly came here to appreciate it and couldn't help but write poetry and essays for it. If there were social platforms in the Song Dynasty, the Shuiyue Cave would definitely make it onto the popular spot list to update the moment. Especially during the dog days when it "steams on top and boils on the bottom", when walking into this cave of the nature to spend your summer holiday, you will be greeted by a refreshing breeze, which is even cooler than blowing an air conditioner.

The Shuiyue Cave is located to the west of the South Peak, at the foot of Rosy Cloud Ridge.

In front of the cave is a quiet small courtyard surrounded by stone bricks, with dense shade from trees. The horizontal banner at the door reads: Shuiyue Cave.

Walking along the stone path to the front of the cave, there is also a square spring pool at the entrance, where small fish play. Across the stone beam on the pool and further into the cave, it suddenly becomes spacious and bright. The entire cave is about 60 meters long, with two entrances separated by a natural giant rock in the middle.

When in the cave, the bubbling of springs can indeed be heard. There are also stone tables and benches placed next to it, which are placed in the best position for listening to the clear and refreshing spring music, providing visitors with a rest to listen to the spring. It is said that if it rains, the melody played on this natural stringed instrument will be even more passionate and moving.

This may be the most enjoyable cave in Hangzhou. Who was the first to name it? This guy's name was Zheng Xie, a "super academic genius" of the Northern Song Dynasty. At the age of 31, he participated in the imperial examination and achieved great success. He won the first place in the imperial examination and was designated as the "Number One Scholar of Loyalty and Filial Piety" by Emperor Renzong of Song. After entering the officialdom, Zheng Xie had always been an honest and upright official. In the second year of Xining period of the Northern Song Dynasty (1069), he was demoted from the governor of Kaifeng to the governor of Hangzhou due to his opposition to Wang Anshi's reform. Feeling depressed, he came here with friends to relieve boredom. Faced with the mystical scenery of "water and clear sound in the cave", he was inspired and named it "Shuiyue Cave". Regarding the naming, Zheng Xie's good friend Wang Fuzhi recorded it and engraved it in the cave.

After Zheng Xie was transferred from Hangzhou to Qingzhou (now Qingzhou City, Shandong Province) for a year, Hangzhou welcomed another academic genius "mayor" — Su Dongpo.

In 1071, as soon as Su Shi arrived in Hangzhou to take office, he came to Manjuelong for sightseeing, and one of the scenic spots for updating the moment was the Shuiyue Cave. With great enthusiasm, he wrote an article entitled "Notes on the Shuiyue Cave": "There is a water cave with music in the southeast of Qiantang. Springs flow in rocks and produce a variety of natural rhythms." As natural limestone can play a good role in amplifying sound, nearly a thousand years ago, the spring water here is the music rhythm.

It seems that nowadays people are accustomed to calling it Shuile Cave, pronounced the character "乐" as "le" (literal meaning "happy"), but the correct pronunciation should be "yue" (literal meaning "music"). In order to enjoy this wonderful "water music", many literati were invited by Su Shi to observe and explore in the cave. Shen Fu, who wrote *Six Records of a Floating Life*, Lin Shu, a famous modern writer, and Huang Yi, one of the Eight Masters of Xiling, came here to update the moment and recite poems.

Gao Lian, a health-living expert in the Ming Dynasty, was very good at exploring niche scenic spots. He specifically included the writing "Listening to Springs after the Rain in Shuiyue Cave" in his health-living book *Gaolian's Appreciation in Autumn of Eight Essays on Life Preservation*.

The literati left numerous comments on the rock walls around the spring pool, but due to the passage of time, most of them have been eroded. What can be seen now are mostly from the late Qing Dynasty to the Republic of China, such as "natural sound of stringed instrument" "listening to musical instrument without strings" "high mountains and flowing water" "clear Buddhist music", etc.

In 1922, the elder brother of Chinese painting master Zhang Daqian, Zhang Shanzi, who was famous for his tiger paintings, came to the Shuiyue Cave with his brothers on pleasure and left an inscription: "Zhang Shanzi from Han'an and his brothers Licheng, Wenxiu, Daqian, and Junshou came here on pleasure." A few years later, the renowned calligrapher and painter Wu Hufan also took his lover Shi Wanqiu on an autumn trip to the Shuiyue Cave, and later wrote a poem to praise it: "Left with us is an exquisite courtyard, as well as a running spring; listening to the voice of the sea, pearl-like drops splashing in the rain".

In addition to being able to hear the babbling of spring water, there have been many different identity labels in the history of the Shuiyue Cave. The earliest one, which is its predecessor, was the Xiguan Purification Zen Temple built by Qian Hongzuo, the King of Wuyue in the Five Dynasties. On the mountain stone next to the Shuiyue Cave, there is an inscription called "Records of the Stone Statue of the Newly-built Ziyan Zen Temple for National Stability", which records the origin of the Xiguan Purification Zen Temple and describes it as "establishing goodness and creating blessings are all convenient doors; raising and lowering heads are all the way back".

In 1179, Emperor Xiaozong of Song rewarded this place to his eunuch Li Li, and afterwards rebuilt the Buddhist temple and expanded the gardens and ponds. During the reign of Emperor Ningzong of the Song Dynasty, the temple was abandoned and the Shuiyue Cave became the private garden of the Prince Yang, who was Yang Yizhong, a native of Yuanping in Shanxi Province. He came from a prestigious family and was a descendant of the "Yang Family of Generals". He was a great general of the Southern Song Dynasty and had made outstanding military achievements. Besides, he was once a batter companion of Yue Fei, and it was he who turned the Shuiyue Cave into a popular scenic spot at that time. He also had a "black history", that is, he was ordered by Qin Hui to trap Yue Fei on Mount Lu and was arranged to supervise the execution of Yue Fei.

In his book *The Old Stories of Hangzhou*, Zhou Mi mentioned that the Ciming Hall of the Shuiyue Cave was bestowed upon the Prince Yang, and later shifted to Jia Pingzhang. The mountain rocks of the cave are exquisitely beautiful, in which sound could be heard, hence the name. At that time, the Shuiyue Cave was Yang Yizhong's private garden, built with stones and pavilions, and had an elegant structure. Later on, this place became silted up over time and gradually became barren. Jia Sidao, a Prime Minister of the Southern Song Dynasty, was also very interested in this place, so he spent a lot of money to buy and renovate it. As a result, the Shuiyue Cave was able to restore its original appearance.

During the Southern Song Dynasty, the Shuiyue Cave underwent several changes in ownership, and its history of revival was recorded by Zhang Dai, the first guy to deeply explore West Lake in the late Ming Dynasty, in his article "Rosy Cloud in the Stone House" in *The West Lake Dream*.

留云谷
Liuyun Valley

景行古桥
Jingxing Ancient Bridge

雪中的杨公堤隐秀桥
Snowy Yinxiu Bridge on Yanggong
Causeway

杨公堤仅剩的古桥

在过去很长一段时间，杨公堤一直叫西山路。相比车水马龙的北山街和南山路，很多人更喜欢静谧野趣的西山路。这里能看到一汪西湖水的另一面，少了明媚奔放，多了和顺矜持。

杨公堤上有六座桥，跟苏堤"六吊桥"呼应，合称"西湖十二桥"。为了有所区分，这六座桥被称为"里六桥"。2003年，西湖综合保护工程中重修了"里六桥"，西山路也重新叫回了杨公堤。

实际上，最早的杨公堤并不在今天的位置。花港公园里藏着一座单孔石拱桥，始建于明代，经清代重修后，一直留存至今，叫作"景行古桥"。

景行古桥所在的位置，就是当年的杨公堤。这座"低调"了两三百年的古桥，是"初代"杨公堤六座古桥中仅剩的一座。

杨公堤位于西湖以西，是在明代"杭州市长"杨孟瑛主持下修筑的。堤上六座桥，自北向南分别为：环璧、流金、卧龙、隐秀、景行、浚源。这六个名字并不是杨孟瑛所取，而是后来得名的。

景行古桥的位置不太好找，这大概也是它低调了这么多年的原因之一。

从杨公堤拐进花港公园西门，走过一个木质水景平台，沿着湖边走，一路清幽，鲜少有游人。直到看到一个立着"杨公堤"题刻的碑亭，景行古桥就在不远处，藏在一片葱茏的草木中间。

景行古桥与西湖国宾馆和苏堤隔水相望，整座古桥长 6 米、宽 2.5 米，外观斑驳古朴。远远望去，古桥有点像一个很大的"水泥管口"，走近细看，才能感受到岁月在石板上留下的痕迹。这座桥始建于明代，现桥为清代重建，算起来，它已经在这里静静躺了两三百年。虽然看起来像一位垂暮老人，但"身子骨"还是十分硬朗的。

为什么叫景行桥？据《西湖游览志》记载，过去在这座桥边上有一个三贤祠，供人们仰慕先贤。《诗经》有"高山仰止，景行行止"的句子，景行指的是宽阔的大道，引申为行为正大光明、品行崇高，景行桥由此得名。

2007 年，在三评西湖十景时，杨公堤入选，这一景定名"杨堤景行"。

景行古桥还有个名字叫"金行桥"，在东侧桥楣上刻有"金行桥"三个字，其中，"金行"两个字比较清晰醒目，"桥"字已经相对模糊了。

藏于西湖深处的景行古桥，和现在的杨公堤六桥隔湖相望，仿佛穿越时空。

杨公堤上的这六座桥，被网友戏称为"过山车六兄弟"，因为每座桥都有很大的坡度，所以车辆行驶过桥时，会有失重感。杨公堤也因此成了杭州人心中著名的"西湖过山车"路线。

前段时间，意外走红的 194 路公交车，也是因为它的行驶路线正好贯穿杨公堤六桥；加上公交车体积大、轴距长的特点，游人搭乘时会比一般的私家车有更明显的失重感。如果路上不堵车，司机师傅心情也不错，这一路上乘客都能享受到翻倍的快乐。

桥上是惊心动魄的起起伏伏，桥下则可以优哉游哉地泛舟西湖。

说起杨公堤上的桥，当然也绕不开"杨公"本人。

同样是杭州"老市长"，同样在西湖上修筑了一条堤，虽然杨孟瑛的名号远不如白居易"市长"和苏轼"市长"深入人心，但他造福一方的功德政绩却能与两位前任"市长"比肩。

明代田汝成在《西湖游览志余》中写道："西湖开浚之绩，古今尤著者，白乐天、苏子瞻、杨温甫三公而已。"意思是说，西湖从形成开始，有不少人都来治理疏浚过，但在他看来，古往今来只有三人功绩显著，即白居易、苏东坡和杨孟瑛（字温甫）。

明弘治十六年（1503），杨孟瑛调任杭州太守，当时的西湖因长久废而不治，已严重淤塞，一些富豪贵族趁机占湖为田，湖面萎缩，湖水渐少。昔日"水光潋滟晴方好"的秀美景致已不复存在。杨孟瑛见到这样的场景，下定决心要疏浚西湖，恢复西湖原貌。他为了说服朝廷，愤而上书，写了洋洋洒洒的万字奏折，力排众议。

杨孟瑛展现出超群的魄力，于明正德三年（1508）开始疏浚西湖，耗时152天。他命人拆去私人河荡，拆毁田亩3481亩，浚湖挖出的淤泥和葑草被分成两部分：一部分置于苏堤上，加高拓宽苏堤，将其填高了二丈（约6.6米），拓宽了五丈三尺（约17.6米），两岸遍植杨柳，使苏堤重新恢复了"六桥烟柳"的固有景色；另一部分则"搬顿西山涯岸，筑成外堤"，作用是"以为界限，使人永远不得再图侵占"。

这条"外堤"，便是最早的"杨公堤"。它始于栖霞岭，绕丁家山直至南山，将西湖湖西山水和众多古迹有机地联系在一起。它与苏堤大致平行，并仿苏堤建有六座桥来连通水域。经过杨孟瑛主持疏浚后的西湖，恢复了唐宋时的湖光山色，南北交通也便利了许多。

但是杨孟瑛这大刀阔斧的一系列行动，得罪了太多的豪绅权贵，第二年就被调离了杭州。杭州人为了感谢这位好市长，把杨孟瑛疏浚西湖时修筑的"外堤"称为"杨公堤"，以此纪念他。

数百年后的杨公堤旁，大片法国梧桐树冠如云，交叠在一起，绿荫蔽日，即使是夏季，感觉也非常凉爽。

杨公堤上串联起的景点很多，包括曲院风荷、金沙港、花圃、茅家埠、乌龟潭、三台梦迹、浴鹄湾和花港观鱼等。

还有一处摄影爱好者钟爱的"秘密基地"，人们在这里可以拍日出日落、四季风光，非常出片。大家把这里称为"神舟基地"，在导航软件中也能找到这里的定位。

除了心旷神怡的风景，杨公堤上还有丰富的历史文化遗迹，其中有两处都与京剧名伶盖叫天有关。

一个是流金桥下赵公堤上的盖叫天旧居"燕南寄庐"。另一个是盖叫天的墓，位于杨公堤旁丁家山上。沿着一条石径上坡，有一座慕侠亭，石柱上刻有对联"英名盖世三叉口，杰作惊天十字坡"。《三岔口》和《十字坡》是盖叫天最有名的两出武戏，这是当时他在上海演出时，海派书画名家吴湖帆为他书写的楹联。横批"学到老"三字，是黄宾虹90岁时写给盖叫天的。

晚清才子赵之谦也长眠此地。赵之谦出生在浙江绍兴，从小是街坊邻居眼中的"神童"，据说他两岁便能挥笔写字。长大后，凭借过人的绘画天赋，他一步步走上艺术巅峰，成为晚清艺术史上最重要的"全能"艺术家之一。在篆刻领域，吴昌硕、齐白石等人都曾受到他的影响。赵之谦的人生停留在了56岁那年，他在江西溘然长逝。后来，亲友们众筹出资，将他的灵柩运回杭州，葬在了丁家山。

既有人文历史，也有无限风光，既有古韵意趣，又有蓬勃朝气，这就是杨公堤。

骑行的游客在杨公堤隐秀桥驻足赏景
Cyclists Pause at Yinxiu Bridge to Enjoy the Scenery

杨公堤，"神舟基地"
The Tranquil Haven of Anchored Boats by Yanggong Causeway

景行古桥
Jingxing Ancient Bridge

The Last Ancient Bridge
on Yanggong Causeway

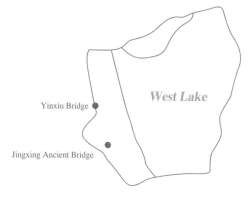

For a long time in the past, Yanggong Causeway was called Xishan Road. Compared to the bustling Beishan Street and Nanshan Road, many people prefer the quiet and wild Xishan Road. Here, you can see the other side of the West Lake water, which is less bright and unrestrained, and more peaceful and reserved.

There are six bridges on Yanggong Causeway, echoing the "Six Stone Arch Bridges" of Sudi Causeway, collectively known as "Twelve Bridges of West Lake". To distinguish them, these six are called "Inner Six Bridges". In 2003, "Inner Six Bridges" were rebuilt by the West Lake Comprehensive Protection Project, and Xishan Road was renamed Yanggong Causeway.

In fact, the earliest Yanggong Causeway was not in its current location. There is a single arch stone bridge hidden in Huagang Park, which was first built in the Ming Dynasty and has been preserved to this day after being rebuilt in the Qing Dynasty. It is called the "Jingxing Ancient Bridge".

The location of Jingxing Ancient Bridge is Yanggong Causeway at that time. This low-key ancient bridge, which has been hidden for two or three hundred years, is the only remaining one among the six ancient bridges of the "first generation" of Yanggong Causeway.

Yanggong Causeway is located west of West Lake and was built under the leadership of Yang Mengying, the "Mayor of Hangzhou" in the Ming Dynasty. There are six bridges on the embankment, from north to south: Huanbi, Liujin, Wolong, Yinxiu, Jingxing, and Junyuan. These six names were not given by Yang Mengying, but were later named.

The location of Jingxing Ancient Bridge is not easy to find, which is probably one of the reasons why it has been low-key for so many years.

From Yanggong Causeway right into the west gate of Huagang Park and past a wooden water platform, you will be greeted by the quiet and secluded road along the lake. Rarely could the visitors be seen on the way until a pavilion with the inscription "Yanggong Causeway" stands. Not far away comes Jingxing Ancient Bridge, which is hidden among lush vegetation.

Jingxing Ancient Bridge faces the West Lake State Guesthouse and Sudi Causeway across the water. The whole ancient bridge is 6 meters long and 2.5 meters wide, with a mottled and antique appearance. From the distance, the ancient bridge looks a bit like a large "cement pipe mouth". Only by approaching and examining closely can one sense the traces left by time on the stone slab. This bridge was first built in the Ming Dynasty and was rebuilt in the Qing Dynasty. In total, it has been quietly lying here for two to three hundred years. Although it looks like an aged in its twilight years, its physical body is still very strong.

Then, why is it called Jingxing Bridge? According to the *West Lake Tourist Chronicles*, there used to have "Three Sages Temple" by this bridge, where people admired the ancestors. In the *Book of Songs*, there is a sentence that goes, "One's moral, if compared to a towering mountain, makes one revere; if compared to a smooth avenue, attracts one to follow". "Jingxing" refers to a wide avenue, which is extended to mean upright and noble behavior, and Jingxing Bridge is named after it.

In 2007, during the three evaluations of Ten Scenic Spots of West Lake, Yanggong Causeway was selected and named "Historical Reflections on Governor Yang Causeway".

Jingxing Ancient Bridge also has a name called "Jinxing Bridge". The three characters "Jin Xing Bridge" are engraved on the east side of the bridge eyebrow. Among them, the two characters "Jin Xing" are relatively clear and eye-catching, while the character "Bridge" has become relatively vague.

Jingxing Ancient Bridge hidden deep in West Lake faces six bridges of the current Yanggong Causeway across the lake, as if they were crossing time and space.

These six bridges are referred to by netizens as the "roller coaster six brothers". As every bridge has a steep slope, there is a sense of weightlessness when vehicles cross the bridge. Yanggong Causeway has thus become a famous "West Lake roller coaster" route in the mind of Hangzhou people.

Recently, the unexpected popularity of bus Route 194 is also due to its running through six bridges of Yanggong Causeway. Thanks to the characteristics of large volume and long wheelbase of buses, they have a more obvious sense of weightlessness than ordinary private cars. If there is no traffic jam on the road and the driver is in a good mood, the whole journey will be doubly happy.

On the bridge, there are thrilling ups and downs, while under the bridge, one can leisurely enjoy boating on West Lake.

When it comes to the bridges over Yanggong Causeway, Governor Yang of Hangzhou is bound to be mentioned.

Yang Mengying, who was also the "old mayor" of Hangzhou and built a causeway on West Lake, is far less well-known than Mayor Bai Juyi and Mayor Su Shi. However, his achievements in benefiting local people are comparable to those of two former mayors.

In the Ming Dynasty, Tian Rucheng wrote in his book *Miscellaneous Records of West Lake Tourism*: "Only Bai Letian , Su Zizhan and Yang wenfu have made unparalle led achievements in dredging the West Lake in ancient and modern times." Which means that since the formation of West Lake, many people had come to govern and dredge it, but in his opinion, only three made significant achievements throughout history: Bai Juyi, Su Dongpo, and Yang Mengying (courtesy name Wenfu).

In 1503, Yang Mengying was transferred to the position of Hangzhou governor. At that time, West Lake had been abandoned for a long time and had become severely silted up. Some wealthy aristocrats took advantage of the situation to occupy the lake as farmlands, causing the shrinking of the lake surface and the decrease of the amount of water. The once beautiful scenery of "the brimming waves delight the eyes on sunny days" no longer exists. Yang Mengying saw such a scene and angrily reported to the throne. In order to persuade the court, he wrote a lengthy memorial of more than ten thousand words against the public opinion, making up his mind to dredge West Lake and restore its water surface.

In the meantime, Yang Mengying demonstrated extraordinary courage. In 1508, he began dredging West Lake, which took 152 days. He ordered to demolish private riverbanks and 3,481 *mu* of farmlands. The silt and humus excavated from the dredging were divided into two parts. One part was placed on Sudi Causeway, which was heightened and widened by two *zhang* (unit of length measurement, approximately 6.6 meters) and five *zhang* and three *chi* (unit of length measurement, approximately 17.6 meters) respectively. Willow trees were planted on both sides, and Sudi Causeway restored the natural scenery of the "Six Bridges in Misty Willows". The other part was carried to the edge of the Xishan Hill and built into an outer embankment, with the purpose of "serving as a boundary so that it could never be occupied".

This "outer embankment" is the earliest "Yanggong Causeway". Starting from Qixia Ridge, winding around Dingjiashan to Nanshan Hill, it neatly connects the scenery of West Lake and numerous historical sites. In addition, it roughly parallels with Sudi Causeway and has six bridges built to connect the water area by imitating Sudi Causeway. After being dredged by Yang Mengying, West Lake has regained its picturesque scenery from the Tang and Song dynasties, and transportation between the north and south has become much more convenient.

However, Yang Mengying's series of bold actions offended too many wealthy and powerful gentries, and he was transferred out of Hangzhou the following year. Hangzhou locals, in order to show their gratitude to this good governor, named the "outer embankment" built by him during the dredging of West Lake as "Yanggong Causeway" to commemorate him.

Hundreds of years later, by Yanggong Causeway, a large area of French Wutong tree crowns, in the shape of clouds, overlap together with its green shade blocking the sun. At this time, waves of coolness bring the comfort to every passer-by.

There are many scenic spots linked on Yanggong Causeway, including Breeze-ruffled Lotus at Quyuan Garden, Jinsha Port, Hangzhou Flower Nursery, Maojiabu, Turtle Pond, Dream Trail of Santai Hill, Yuhu Bay, and Viewing Fish at Flower Pond, etc.

There is also a beloved "secret site" for photography enthusiasts, where you can capture sunrise, sunset, and the changing seasons, making it a great place to shoot. Everyone calls this place the "Satellite Launch Base for Shenzhou", and its location can also be found in navigation software.

Apart from the refreshing scenery, Yanggong Causeway also has rich historical and cultural relics, two of which are related to the famous Peking Opera performer Gai Jiaotian.

The former residence of Gai Jiaotian, "Yannan Jilu", is located on Zhaogong Causeway under Liujin Bridge. The other is Gai Jiaotian's tomb, located on Dingjiashan next to Yanggong Causeway. Along a stone path uphill, there is a pavilion for admiring the hero, with the inscription on the stone pillar "Great reputation At the Crossroad, amazing masterpiece in The Cross Slope". *At the Crossroad* and *The Cross Slope* are two of Gai Jiaotian's most famous martial arts plays. These were couplets written by the famous Shanghai style calligrapher and painter Wu Hufan for him during his performance in Shanghai. The horizontal inscription "Never too old to learn" was written by Huang Binhong to Gai Jiaotian at the age of ninety.

There is one more thing. Zhao Zhiqian, a talented scholar of the late Qing Dynasty, also died here. He was born in Shaoxing, Zhejiang Province. From a young age, he was regarded as a "prodigy" by his neighbors and was said to be able to write at the age of two. As he grew up, with his exceptional talent for painting, he gradually reached the art peak and became one of the most important "versatile" artists in the art history of late Qing. In the field of seal carving, Wu Changshuo, Qi Baishi and others had been influenced by him. Zhao Zhiqian's life ended at the age of 56 when he passed away suddenly in Jiangxi. Later, relatives and friends raised funds through crowdfunding and transported his coffin back to Hangzhou for burial on Dingjiashan.

This is the secret of Yanggong Causeway to attract the public attention — both culturally and historically presented with ancient charm and vitality, as well as indefinite scenery.

虎跑公园，"梦虎"雕塑
"Dreaming Tiger" Sculpture, Hupao Park

虎跑径旁，水杉耸立，泉水淙淙
Hupao Trail Lined with Towering Water Spruce Trees in a Murmuring Spring

深山古寺里的"绿野仙踪"

西湖

虎跑 ●

明代高濂写过一本《四时幽赏录》，列举了杭州人一年四季所做的"闲"事。其中，春天最该做的一件事，便是到虎跑，"高卧山中，沉酣新茗一月"。

用虎跑泉水冲沏一壶龙井新茶，然后在山中躺上一个月，真是想想都惬意。生活在快节奏中的当代人，对古人的这种玩法只有羡慕的份，但认真走一走虎跑，却不算是件难事。我们也可以在这个有山有泉、绿意盎然的公园里感受自然，找到久违的"松弛感"。

虎跑公园距离杭州市区不远，门口就是西湖景区最繁忙的道路之一：虎跑路。但即便是热闹的节假日，这里也常常被游客忽略。虎跑公园不是人们春游踏青的首选地，它始终保持低调和静谧，像隐居山林的世外高人。

它的美，被很多人低估了。"深山藏古寺"，说的就是虎跑。这里位于白鹤峰下，四面环山，原是唐代大慈寺和它的寺庙园林，后改名大慈定慧禅寺。明清时，经数次改建、扩建，形成两组寺院，除了定慧寺，又增加一座虎跑寺。因地形高低错落，山上林木葱茏蓊郁，这座寺庙园林景观极为优美。

当你迈进山门的那一刻，外面车水马龙的喧嚣仿佛瞬间消失，浓厚的绿意扑面而来，仿佛踏进"绿野仙踪"。脚步慢下来，心也跟着静下来。

进门是一条青石板铺就的林荫道，两侧被数不清的参天水杉围绕。这条林荫道名为虎跑径，一路延伸至虎跑山间，其间坡度缓缓上升，如果夏天来这里漫步，会越走越清凉，是纳凉的好地方。

一路上泉水叮咚、溪水潺潺，池塘里有锦鲤嬉戏，这个季节能看到金黄色的"三寸金莲"点缀其中，还有小瀑布湍流而下。一条虎跑径，处处是生机。

途中，你会遇到一对威风凛凛的石老虎，它是由艺术大师韩美林创作的。虎跑有不少"老虎"，这两只算是"迎客虎"，像是公园的"守护神"。

前行大概几百米，含晖亭出现在眼前。过去，它所在的位置曾建有虎跑寺的里山门。山门外原来还有成对的动物石像，是 2008 年自含晖亭附近出土的一对赑屃（bì xì）石像。

赑屃，是龙生九子中的第六位，中国老底子祥兽，象征长寿吉祥，千秋不衰；据说善驮重物，常成为石碑的基座，是任劳任怨的负重者。含晖亭前的这组赑屃，背上的石碑已然不存，但神兽本体依然安好，挂着很治愈的微笑。

沿着泊云桥穿过日月池，就到了历史上虎跑寺与定慧寺的交叉处。虎跑曾有过三次大毁大建，最后一次重建，是清雍正四年（1726），距今已有近300 年历史。目前虎跑公园内这一系列建筑都采用清式民间朴素的山林寺院类风格。

虎跑公园建筑群为纵横线上分布两个寺院的格局，正前方东西走向的一系列建筑是明代寺院扩建的"上院"，也就是后来虎跑寺建筑的中轴线。

上山的路有两条。其中一条可以通向虎跑公园内的一处野餐地——一个木质大平台。这里鸟语花香，绿荫如盖，即使是大太阳的日子也不会觉得晒。有人早晨来这里打打太极拳，有人在这里铺开垫子做春日野餐。在这个平台上，人们甚至都不想刷手机，闭目冥想，感觉每个毛孔都在大口呼吸着清新空气。

顺着长台阶，能看到"虎跑泉"照壁这一方向的，是历史上早期定慧禅寺的中轴线。拾级而上，便看见围墙上写的"天下第三泉"五个大字。

虎跑公园里最出名的就是虎跑泉水。这也是虎跑特有的"大自然的馈赠"，市民、游客来这里游玩一趟，还能免费带走这份"特色纪念品"。

虎跑水的形成当然不是如传说中的那样，是两只老虎"跑（刨）地作穴"

刨出来的，它和这里群山环抱的自然条件有着密切的关系。虎跑泉眼所在的滴翠崖，处在三面山岭的包围之下，形成一个马蹄形的汇水池。它四周的群山都是透水性较差的石英砂岩，形成了良好的地形和供水条件。地下水通过石英砂岩裂隙源源不断地流出，形成了地质学上的"裂隙泉"。

从唐代建寺算起，虎跑泉已经流淌了1000多年。现在，每天拖着大容量空桶来虎跑取水，成了不少"老杭州"开启一天幸福感的"规定动作"，为了这杯甘甜，有些人甚至坚持了十来年。

在泉眼处，取水的人自觉排队，日子久了自然成了熟面孔，互相寒暄几句。若是碰到拿矿泉水瓶想接水尝鲜的外地游客，大家还会主动让道，让"小瓶先行"。

前阵子，网络上流传一个视频。说的是一位上海姑娘为了用虎跑泉水泡新茶，凌晨4点出门，坐高铁来杭州，到虎跑装了一大瓶泉水，返程；中午12点半，终于在上海家里喝上了用虎跑泉水泡的茶。有网友感叹："这样的人生才是真的松弛啊！"

虎跑泉为什么出名？这主要是乾隆皇帝的功劳，"天下第三泉"就是他钦定的。据清代陆以湉《冷庐杂识》记载，乾隆每次出巡，喜欢带一只精制银斗，用来"精量各地泉水"，精心称重后，按水的比重从轻到重排出优次。他定北京玉泉山水为"天下第一泉"，作为宫廷御用水；济南珍珠泉斗重一两二厘，无锡惠山泉、杭州虎跑泉各重一两四厘——天下排名前三的泉水就这样诞生了。

由于虎跑泉水表面张力很大，用杯子将水放满，水面渐渐高出杯面2—3毫米也不会外溢。如果将分币轻轻放入水中，它会浮在水面上而不下沉，十分有趣。这也是虎跑泉的神奇之处。在"叠翠轩"内就设有几组"试泉台"，游客可以在现场投钱体验。

进入虎跑公园深处，是一处精致的庭院。按照中国传统的风水园林学，在这样一块风水宝地，自然少不了高人坐镇。

一百多年前，李叔同选择在虎跑断食17天，因为这里足够清雅幽静，又有天然泉水。断食是一种什么样的体验？李叔同写下了出家前唯一一本日记体作品《断食日志》，他在日志中写道："十一月二十二日，决定断食。祷诸大神

"乾隆取水"雕塑
The Group Statue of "Emperor Qianlong's Escorted Wagon Fetching Water from Hupao Spring"

虎跑泉取水口
The Water Fetching Site at Hupao Spring

之前，神诏断食，故决定之……"可见，他从开始就对这次断食抱着慎重与认真的态度，而且准备得十分充分。

断食的方法也有讲究。根据日志记载，李叔同从 12 月 1 日开始，前 5 日为半断食，渐减食量；中间 7 日全断食，只饮水和果汁；后 5 日开始逐渐恢复饮食。所以，这 17 日的断食并不是全程不吃不喝，而是一个循序渐进的过程。

日志中，李叔同除了将自己的生活细节和每天的生理变化进行详细记录之外，还写了许多有趣之事。比如，他在梦里尝试跳高，轻松跳跃甚至腾飞于天上。醒来后，从不做体育运动、更没跳过高的李叔同思考："这是因为我腹中过于虚空导致的吗？"

后来，李叔同在虎跑定慧寺正式出家为僧，法名演音，号弘一。

虎跑后山，有一座弘一法师塔。1953 年春，丰子恺游虎跑时得知弘一法师部分灵骨从福建泉州送至此处，却多年无碑志，丰子恺便决心出资安葬灵骨并建塔。2023 年，弘一法师舍利塔被评为浙江省级文物保护单位。

在弘一法师李叔同之前，虎跑还有另一位高僧，他就是南宋传奇僧人济公。虎跑公园内有济公殿、济公塔院等建筑，这里也是杭州市非遗"济公传说"的传承基地。

《净慈寺志》中记载："道济……荼毗，舍利如雨，葬虎跑塔中。"在济公殿后的济公塔院，相传是济公圆寂葬骨之处，民国五年（1916）前后，虎跑寺建造虎跑佛祖藏殿后，又在虎跑寺院内建造了济公塔院，后来，以扮演济公出名的著名演员游本昌捐资加以修葺扩建，形成了目前的规模。墙壁上的一组济公像石刻，就是以游本昌饰演的"鞋儿破、帽儿破"的济公形象为原型的。

再往上，还有一处很多人都不一定到过的观音殿，此处算是虎跑公园里的"冷门"景点。据《西湖新志》记载，清同治十一年（1872），僧人普缘募建观音殿五楹。后来，观音殿几经毁坏，直到 2017 年，才重新修建完成。这里是全国唯一一处以陶瓷为主要载体的观音展陈，而殿内的观音主像也是目前全国最大的一体成型的观音瓷塑像。

前面说到过虎跑公园里有不少"老虎"。除了虎跑径上的两只，更出名的一只石老虎在虎跑泉原始出水口滴翠崖。这是杭州人的童年回忆，也是曾经红极一时的"网红打卡点"，很多人家里都有一张跟石老虎合影的照片。

这只石虎是在 20 世纪 50 年代由民间艺人陈鹤亭先生创作的。随着时光流逝，近古稀之年的石虎"皮肤"褪色，牙齿脱落。

2023 年下半年，杭州西湖风景名胜区钱江管理处对这只有些"年迈"的石虎进行了修复，修旧如旧。现在看到的石虎已经是修复完成的，看起来精神抖擞，"脱落"的牙齿也补上了，根根胡须清晰可辨，威风凛凛。

跟这只明星石虎差不多出名的，还有虎跑公园里的"梦虎"雕塑，创作于 1983 年。"虎跑梦泉"被评为"新西湖十景"之一时，这组雕塑就是其中一景。

很多人会误以为那位屈臂托腮、微闭双目，侧卧在山崖之中的僧人是济公，其实这是唐代的寰中禅师。这也是虎跑由来的传说。相传，寰中禅师云游到杭州时，看中这块地方景色佳美，便想结庵于此，但这里远离湖泊，没有水源，他只好遗憾放弃。日有所思，夜得一梦，梦中有神人说："南岳童子泉，当遣二虎移来。"次日清晨，禅师果然看见两只老虎刨地作穴，泉水即时涌出，从此就有了"虎跑泉"。

这就是虎跑，林深泉清，一个让人治愈又松弛的所在，一个适合"白日做梦"的地方。

"虎跑泉"照壁
The Screen Wall Inscribed with the Words "Hupao Spring"

虎跑公园，含晖亭、泊云桥和日月池
Hanhui Pavilion, Boyun Bridge and
Riyue Pond at Hupao Park

虎跑公园一角
A Corner of Hupao Park

The "Wizard of Oz" in an Ancient Temple in Deep Mountains

West Lake

Hupao

During the Ming Dynasty, Gao Lian wrote a book called *Record of Four Seasons of Serenity Appreciation*, which listed the "leisure" activities of Hangzhou locals throughout the year. Among them, the most important thing to do in spring is to pay a visit to Hupao, just as the saying goes: "Lying high in the mountains and enjoying the fresh tea for a month".

Brewing a pot of new Dragon Well tea with Hupao spring water, and then lying in the mountains for a month, it's so comforting to think about it. Contemporary generation living in a fast-paced environment may envy the ancient way of leisure-spending, but taking a serious walk and running around Hupao is not difficult. We can also experience nature and find a long-lost sense of relaxation in this park with mountains, springs, and lush greenery.

Hupao Park is not far from the city center of Hangzhou, and at its entrance is one of the busiest roads in the West Lake scenic area: Hupao Road. But even during busy holidays, this place is often overlooked by tourists. Hupao Park is not the first choice for people to go on spring outings. It always maintains a low profile and tranquility, like a reclusive hermit in the mountains and forests.

It's a pity that the beauty of Hupao has been underestimated by many people. The case of ancient temples hidden in deep mountains may be referred to as that of Hupao. This place is located at the foot of the White Crane Peak, surrounded by mountains on all sides. It was originally Daci Temple in the Tang Dynasty together with its affiliated garden, and later renamed Daci Dinghui Zen Temple. During the Ming and Qing dynasties, it underwent several renovations and expansions, forming two groups of temples. Apart from Dinghui Temple, Hupao Temple was added. Due to the uneven terrain and lush forests on the mountains, the garden landscape of this temple is extremely beautiful.

At the moment you step into the temple gate, the hustle and bustle of the traffic outside seems to be instantly silenced, and a strong greenery rushes towards you, as if stepping into the Emerald Palace in "Wizard of Oz." As you slow down your steps, your mind also quiets down.

After entering the door, what catches the eye is a tree-lined avenue paved with bluestone boards, surrounded by countless towering water spruce trees on both sides. This tree-lined path is called the Hupao Trail, which extends all the way to Hupao Hill, with a gradually rising slope. If you come here for a stroll in summer, it will become cooler as you walk and is surely a good place to cool off.

All the way along the Hupao Trail tinkles the spring water, gurgles the stream, and koi fish are playing carefreely in the pond. In this season, you can see golden "small but exquisite lotuses" embellished among them, as well as small waterfalls rushing down. To put it simple, the Hupao Trail is full of vitality.

On the way, you will encounter a pair of majestic stone tigers created by the art master Han Meilin. There are many "tigers" in Hupao, and these two are considered "welcoming tigers", like the "guardian gods" of the park.

About a few hundred meters ahead, there comes Hanhui Pavilion in front. In the past, the location of it stood the inner temple gate of Hupao Temple. Besides, there used to be a pair of animal stone statues outside the temple gate, which are actually a pair of "Bi Xi" unearthed near Hanhui Pavilion in 2008.

"Bi Xi", the sixth of the nine sons born to the dragon, is an auspicious beast in China, symbolizing longevity and auspiciousness. It is said to be good at carrying heavy objects and often serves as the base of stone tablets. It is a burden bearing being which works tirelessly. This pair of "Bi Xi" in front of Hanhui Pavilion no longer bears the stone tablet on their backs, but the divine beast itself is still fine, with a very healing smile on its face.

Passing through the Sun Moon Pool along Boyun Bridge, you will arrive at the intersection of Hupao Temple and Dinghui Temple in history. In fact, Hupao has undergone three major demolitions and constructions, with the last reconstruction taking place in the fourth year of the Yongzheng reign of the Qing Dynasty (1726), which has a history of nearly 300 years. At present, the style of this series of buildings in Hupao Park is the simple mountain and forest temple style of Qing Dynasty folk architecture.

The architectural complex of Hupao Park consists of two temples arranged vertically and horizontally. The series of buildings running east to west in front of it are the "Upper Courtyard" of the Ming Dynasty temple expansion, which later became known as the central axis of Hupao Temple architecture.

There are two uphill roads. One leads to a picnic area, a large wooden platform in Hupao Park. Here, birds sing and flowers bloom, and the canopy green shade is like a cover. Even on sunny days, you won't feel sunburned. Some locals come here in the morning to practice Tai Chi, while others lay out mats for a spring picnic. On this platform, you don't even want to scroll on your phone, but close your eyes and meditate, feeling like every pore is breathing fresh air.

Following the long steps, you can see a screen wall facing the gate inscribed with "Hupao Spring", which is the central axis of the early Dinghui Zen Temple in history. Up the stairs, there come several big Chinese characters on the wall that goes "The Third Spring in the World".

The most famous attraction in Hupao Park is Hupao Spring Water. This is also a unique "gift from nature" of Hupao. Citizens and tourists who come here for a visit can also take away this "special souvenir" for free.

The water formation in Hupao is not the case as rumored — two tigers digging holes in the ground, thus flows out the water. It is closely related to the natural conditions surrounded by mountains here. The Dicui Cliff, where the Hupao Spring is located, is surrounded by three mountain ranges, forming a horseshoe-shaped water collecting pool. The surrounding mountains are made of poorly permeable quartz sandstone, providing good terrain and water supply conditions for its formation. Groundwater continuously flows out through quartz sandstone fissures, forming geological fissure springs.

Since the establishment of the temple in the Tang Dynasty, Hupao Spring has been flowing for over 1,000 years. Nowadays, fetching water with large empty buckets every day has become a routine for many Hangzhou natives to start a day of happiness. Some people have even persisted for more than ten years for this sweet treat.

At the spring, water collectors consciously line up, and as time passes, they naturally become acquaintances and it is quite common for them to exchange a few pleasantries with each other. If tourists from other places holding mineral water bottles want to bring water back to try something new, they are likely to be voluntarily given

济公塔院
Jigong Pagoda Courtyard

李叔同弘一法师纪念馆
Master Hongyi (Li Shutong) Memorial Hall

207

way and endowed with the practice of "small bottle first".

A while ago, there was a video circulating online about a girl from Shanghai who went out at 4 a.m. and took a high-speed train to Hangzhou so as to make new tea with Hupao Spring Water. She filled a large bottle of spring water at Hupao and returned home at 12:30 p.m. Some netizens exclaimed, "This kind of life is really relaxing."

Why is Hupao Spring famous? It is mainly due to the credit of Emperor Qianlong, who designated Hupao Spring as "The Third Spring in the World". According to Lu Yitian's *Miscellaneous Knowledge in Cold House* during the Qing Dynasty, Emperor Qianlong liked to bring a refined silver bucket with him every time he went on a tour, which was used to "measure springs from various places". After careful weighing, the water was ranked from light to heavy according to its specific gravity. In terms of the priority, the water from Beijing Yuquan Mountain was designated as the "No.1 Spring in the World" and used as water for the imperial court. Jinan Pearl Spring weighs one *liang* and two *li* (unit of weight, approximately sixty grams); Wuxi Huishan Spring and Hangzhou Hupao Spring each weigh one *liang* and four *li* (unit of weight, approximately seventy grams). In this way, the top three springs in the world came into being.

Due to the high surface tension of Hupao Spring, it is possible to fill a cup with water and gradually raises the water surface 2−3 millimeters above the cup surface without overflowing. If coins are gently placed in the water, they will float on the surface without sinking, which is very interesting and also the magic of Hupao Spring. There are several sets of "trial spring platforms" inside the "Diecui Pavilion", where tourists can put the coin in the water for experience on site.

In the depths of Hupao Park, there is a profound and exquisite courtyard. According to the traditional Chinese "fengshui" and garden studies, in such a treasured land, it is natural to have a master sitting in.

Over a hundred years ago, Li Shutong chose to go on a 17-day hunger strike at Hupao. As it is elegant and quiet here, and there are also natural springs. Then, what kind of experience is fasting? Li Shutong wrote his only work with diary style before becoming a monk, *Fasting Diary*, in which he wrote: "On 22nd November, I made up my mind to go fasting. Before starting I proyed to the great gods, who decreed fasting, so it was decided..." It can be seen that he had a cautious and serious attitude towards this fasting from the beginning, and was very well prepared.

There are also specific methods for fasting. According to the daily records, Li Shutong started semi-fasting from 1st December and gradually reduced his food intake for the first 5 days; complete fasting for the middle 7 days, only drinking water and fruit juice; and gradually resumed eating from the next 5 days. So, this 17-day fasting is not a complete process of not eating or drinking, but a gradual process.

In the daily records, Li Shutong not only noted down the details of his daily life and physiological changes, but also wrote many interesting things. For example, in his dream, he tried to jump high, effortlessly jumping and even soaring up. After waking up, Li Shutong, who never did sports or jumps too high, thought to himself: Is this because my belly is too empty?

Later, Li Shutong officially became a monk at Dinghui Temple in Hupao, with the Dharma name Yanyin and the pseudonym Hongyi.

Behind the Hupao Mountain, there is a tower of Master Hongyi. In the spring of 1953, Feng Zikai learned while traveling that some of Master Hongyi's spiritual bones had been transported from Quanzhou, Fujian to this place, but there had been no inscriptions for many years. Feng Zikai decided to contribute in burying his ashes and building a pagoda. In 2023, Master Hongyi's Pagoda was awarded as a provincial-level cultural relic protection unit in Zhejiang.

Before Master Hongyi (Li Shutong), there was another eminent monk in Hupao, the legendary monk Jigong in the Southern Song Dynasty. There are Jigong Hall and Jigong Pagoda Courtyard in Hupao Park, which are also the inheritance base of Hangzhou's intangible cultural heritage "Jigong Legend".

According to the *Jingci Temple Chronicles*, "Daoji... cremation, relics like rain, buried in the pagoda of Hupao". The Jigong Pagoda Courtyard behind the Jigong Hall is said to be the burial site of Jigong's passing. Around the fifth year of the Republic of China (1916), after the construction of the Hupao Buddha's Hall at Hupao Temple, the Jigong Pagoda Courtyard was also built inside the temple. Later, the famous actor You Benchang, who was famous for playing Jigong, donated funds to repair and expand it, forming the current scale. The set of stone carvings of the image of Jigong on the wall is based on the character of Jigong played by You Benchang, who impressed the audience deeply by singing "broken shoes and broken hat".

Uphill further, there is a Guanyin Hall that many people may not have checked in, which can be considered as an "unpopular" attraction in Hupao Park. According to the *New Chronicles of West Lake*, in the eleventh year of Tongzhi reign in the Qing Dynasty (1872), monk Puyuan raised funds to build five pillars of the Guanyin Hall. In the long history that followed, it was destroyed several times until it was rebuilt and completed in 2017. This is the only Guanyin exhibition in the country that uses ceramics as the main carrier, and the main statue of Guanyin in the hall is currently the largest integrated Guanyin porcelain statue in the country.

As mentioned earlier, there are many "tigers" in Hupao Park. In addition to the two tigers on the Hupao Trail, the more famous one is a stone tiger that stands at the Dicui Cliff, which is actually the original outlet of the Hupao Spring. This is a childhood memory of Hangzhou locals, and also a once popular "internet famous spot". Many households have a photo of themselves with the stone tiger.

This stone tiger was created in the 1950s by folk artist Mr. Chen Heting. As time goes by, the stone tiger, which is almost in its seventies, has fading "skin" and loses its teeth.

In the second half of 2023, the Qianjiang Management Office of Hangzhou West Lake Scenic Area repaired this somewhat "old" stone tiger, restoring it to its original state. The stone tiger that we see now has been restored and looks energetic. Its "fallen" teeth have also been repaired, and its whiskers are clear and recognizable, exuding a majestic aura.

Similar to this celebrity stone tiger, there is also the "Dreaming Tiger" sculpturein Hupao Park, which was created in 1983. When "Dreaming of Tiger Spring at Hupao Valley" was rated as one of the "New Ten Scenic Spots of West Lake", this set of sculptures become one of the spots in the list.

On many occasions, it is often mistakenly thought by the visitors that the monk lying on the cliff with his arms bent over his cheeks and his eyes slightly closed is Jigong, but in fact, this is Zen Master Huanzhong in the Tang Dynasty, which also derives the legend of Hupao. According to the legend, when Master Huanzhong traveled to Hangzhou, he was impressed by the beautiful scenery of this place and wanted to build a temple here. However, it was far from a lake and had no water source, so he had to give up regretfully. After a deep contemplation about the matter during the day, he had a dream at night, in which a divine person said to him, "There is Tongzi Spring on Mount Heng in Nanyue. We will send two tigers to move it here." The next morning, Zen Master indeed saw two tigers digging holes in the ground, and the spring water immediately gushed out, hence the name "Hupao Spring" (literally meanize "dug by tigers").

This is Hupao with deep forests and clear water. Indeed, it is a place for healing and relaxation, as well as daydreaming.

賞幽景

叠翠轩
Diecui Pavilion

虎跑公园，清音亭
Qingyin Pavilion at Hupao Park

虎跑公园，虎跑泉
Hupao Spring at Hupao Park

虎跑公园，虎跑泉
Hupao Spring at Hupao Park

月轮山下的浙江大学之江校区和六和塔
Yuelun Hill Overlooking Zhejiang
University's Zhijiang Campus and
Liuhe Pagoda Below

西湖边有座以月亮为名的山，六和塔就在它脚下

西湖

月轮山
●

杭州三面环山一面城，群山如屏，守护着如珠似玉的西子湖。

西湖景区诸山，除了大家熟悉的吴山、玉皇山、凤凰山、宝石山、南北高峰，还有一处鲜为人知的所在，很多人可能连它的名字都未必听过——月轮山。

其实月轮山很好找，它紧挨着钱塘江，六和塔就耸立在山下。据《杭州府志》记载，月轮山"以其形圆如月，故名"。

这名字很有武侠气息，也很有诗意，让人忍不住想探究一番。前段时间，我们特地去爬了这座以月亮为名的山。可能是因为身在山中，故而不识其真面目吧，不管从哪个角度看，我们都没看出月圆的形状。

这丝毫不影响月轮山的魅力。我们发现，这里有一条风景绝美的登山路线。经过一番探寻之后，我们不由得感叹，它不应如此寂寞，它的美值得被更多人探索。

农历八月十八，钱江大潮。提起观潮，很多人会想到六和塔，在这里观潮的传统已经风靡了近千年。

六和塔就在月轮山下，它的东南面是钱塘江大桥。一塔一桥，一古一今，与月轮山上的自然环境完美地融合在了一起。

六和塔在民间的知名度远远超过了月轮山。南宋的塔身，元代的塔刹，明代的塔顶，清代的廊檐外观，几经损毁又重建的六和塔，如今呈现给世人的，是历史变迁带来的不同建筑风格的完美融合。

往山上走，从西面的山间小路走到半山腰，还有被称为"杭州最美校园"的浙江大学之江校区。校园依山而建，隐匿在月轮山麓。

浙大之江校区是全国重点文物保护单位，完整保留了20余座历史建筑。地灵而人杰，司徒雷登的弟弟司徒华林在这里当了6年校长，孙中山也曾经亲自到访。之江校区的百余年历史中，还有陈望道、郁达夫、夏承焘、吴晗、朱生豪等名人都在此学习、任教。

这里最出名的建筑，是一座"红房子"。之江校区的前身之江大学，是第一批由外国建筑师主持规划设计的中国高等学校校园，是中国最早具有明显西方校园规划设计特点的高等学府之一，其建筑由西方近代风格糅合东方传统风格而成，以清水红砖砌成。整座建筑呈山字形，围绕最醒目的红色钟楼，左右对称。钟楼原名同怀堂，又名经济学馆，建于民国25年（1936），由《申报》总经理史量才先生家属捐建。

浙大之江校区的这座红色建筑，掩映在月轮山郁郁葱葱的山林里，既有历史感，又十分醒目。《唐山大地震》《左耳》《解密》等众多影视剧，都把这里作为取景地。

月轮山的美，当然不只在以上两处"众所周知"的景点上体现，山巅之上，才是它的"高光"。

月轮山本身海拔不算高，只有153米，但这条线路爬起来却不算轻松——从六和塔景区出发，一路经过辽桥岗、头龙头、大华山、马儿山岗，最后到达虎跑后山的贵人阁。

这一整片的山林区域，都属于月轮山脉。一路走下来，翻山越岭，走走停停，大约需要2个小时。

月轮山登山的主入口，在六和塔景区售票处旁边的六和塔牌楼路附近，游客往往都会直接去六和塔，很少有人会走入这条岔道。在牌楼路右侧靠近公共厕所的一条游步道，就是登山道。

沿路而进，一条小径直入幽远。小径沿着月轮山泉一路修建，泉水淙淙，清澈甘甜。小径中还有两处"取水点"，有不少住在附近的村民，会提着矿泉水桶来这里接泉水。

往里走约 500 米，秀树翠林间出现一片茶园，茶园的右侧有一座牌坊，这里是浙江省重点文物保护单位——龚佳育墓。

龚佳育，杭州人，是清代一位颇有作为的官吏，曾任户部主事、兵部郎中、山东按察使、江南布政使等职。他一生经历 7 次仕途升迁，康熙皇帝曾同时将太常寺卿和光禄寺卿两处主官的位置授予他。一人身兼两个二品大臣之位，可见康熙对他器重有加。

龚佳育也不负众望，为官 30 多年，清廉爱民、奉公守职、不畏权贵、施政有方，深受地方百姓的爱戴。他还是清初著名的藏书家，家中藏书数万卷，学识渊博。

龚佳育墓是目前杭州少见的保存完好的清代士大夫墓葬实例，墓前的华表、牌坊、碑亭、石马、石虎等均完好无损，远远望去，气派威严。

离开龚佳育墓后，便到了辽桥岗，这一段山路坡度较缓，石阶宽度较大，走起来还算是比较轻松的。

从辽桥岗至头龙头的登山步道是一眼望不到尽头的盘道台阶，层层叠叠往上延伸，坡度有点陡，非常难爬。

石阶旁装有一排绿色的扶手栏杆，以辅助游客攀登。虽然如此，但难度系数依然很高，特别是平常不大运动的人，需要很大的勇气才能一步步继续往上走。

"没苦硬吃"，说的可能就是高温天来爬这段台阶路了。到底有多少级台阶？有人数过，有说一共 666 级，还有说一共 686 级。

一步三喘地爬完"666 台阶"就到了一处观景点，站在一块凸起的岩石上，可以眺览整座钱塘江大桥。大桥和江水构成的壮丽画卷在眼前打开，风景确实"666"。

这处山头，叫头龙头，位于月轮山脉的西北面。这是坊间传说中杭州"九龙头"的起点。所谓九龙头，指的是从六和塔西至梵村沿线钱塘江畔的群山总称，山山相连，高低起伏，宛若龙形。头龙头就是第一个山头，浙江大学之江校区校址所在地是二龙头。

继续前行，从头龙头经大华山至马儿山岗，这一段相对"666台阶"要平缓好走不少，视野也很开阔。没有树木遮挡的时候，极目远眺，也是一种享受。

这一路上的最佳取景点，是大华山顶的一块巨石，这里视野开阔，是不少资深爬山爱好者的必打卡点。

站在巨石上，蓝天白云，连绵群山，尽收眼底。看着这样的风景，还能有什么烦恼？心情豁然开朗，整个人会瞬间变得轻松自在。

提醒大家，在这个位置拍照要格外当心，千万不要走到岩石边缘；石头一侧也专门写有"注意安全"四个红色大字。

这条爬山线路的终点是虎跑后山山巅的贵人峰，中途也有分岔路，可以去满觉陇、九溪、理安寺。

去虎跑后山的这条路，仍旧是走不完的台阶，但好在稍有起伏，不算陡峭，加上沿途是郁郁葱葱的山峦、形状规整的翠绿茶园，很容易就会忘记登山的疲劳。

一路走到虎跑后山的贵人峰，就能看到顶上的贵人阁，这是登月轮山脉的另一个惊喜。

这是一座建于2002年的仿古重檐式六角亭，高11.5米，中间设螺旋扶梯，可以登至上层高处观景。这里360°无遮挡，可以同时远眺西湖、钱塘江两岸，玉皇山、南北高峰等群山也近在眼前，视野极佳。

如果不走回头路，从贵人阁下山的游步道还另有两条：一条路程短，但石阶路比较陡峭，需要格外小心一点；另一条路程稍长，但相对平缓。这两条路都可以通往虎跑公园。

头龙头山上俯瞰钱塘江
A View of the Qiantang River from Toulongtou Hill

马儿山岗俯瞰茶园
A View of the Tea Field from Ma'er Hillock

月轮山下的六和塔
Liuhe Pagoda at the Foot of Yuelun Hill

浙江大学之江校区
Zhejiang University's Zhijiang Campus

Moon-Named Hill Overlooking West Lake and Liuhe Pagoda

West Lake

Yuelun Hill
●

Hangzhou is a city surrounded by mountains on three sides, with the peaks forming a screen that cradles West Lake like a pearl.

Among the hills and mountains in the West Lake scenic area—such as Wushan Hill, Yuhang Hill, Phoenix Hill, Baoshi Hill, Northern Peak, and Southern Peak—there is a little-known hill that even many locals may not have heard of: Yuelun Hill ("Full Moon Hill").

Yuelun Hill is easy to spot, standing next to the Qiantang River with Liuhe Pagoda at its foot. According to *the Records of Hangzhou Prefecture*, Yuelun Hill "is named for its full moon shape".

This poetic name seems to be inspired by Chinese wuxia novels enticing tourists to explore it. However, when you see the hill in person, you can't perceive its full moon shape from any angle, perhaps because you can't see the forest for the trees.

Anyway, that does not lessen its poetic charm. There is a hiking route for you to explore its stunning scenery. After your exploration, you'll naturally exclaim that it shouldn't be so solitary and that its beauty deserves more visitors.

The tidal bores of the Qianjiang River occur on the 18th day of the eighth month of the lunar calendar. Many people associate Liuhe Pagoda with tide-watching because it has been a tradition to watch tidal bores from there for nearly a thousand years.

Liuhe Pagoda is located at the base of Yuelun Hill, with Qiantang River Bridge to its southeast. One ancient pagoda and one modern bridge blend perfectly with the natural environment of Yuelun Mountain.

Liuhe Pagoda is much more renowned in folklore than Yuelun Hill. The pagoda features a body from the Southern Song Dynasty, a steeple tip from the Yuan Dynasty, a steeple from the Ming Dynasty, and gallery eaves from the Qing Dynasty. Liuhe Pagoda, having been damaged and rebuilt multiple times, now showcases a blend of different architectural styles shaped by historical changes.

Hike along the trail on the west side of Yuelun Hill up to the mountainside, and you'll see Zhejiang University's Zhijiang Campus, often called "Hangzhou's most beautiful campus". The school is nestled at the foothill of Yuelun Hill, designed to follow the natural contours of the landscape.

Zhijiang Campus is a major historical and cultural site protected at the national level, home to over 20 preserved historical buildings. The campus boasts a rich history. John Leighton Stuart's younger brother, Warren Horton, served as the university's president for six years, and Sun Yat-sen himself visited the campus. Throughout its more than hundred-year history, Zhijiang Campus has hosted many notable figures, including Chen Wangdao, Yu Dafu, Xia Chengtao, Wu Han, and Zhu Shenghao, who have both studied and taught here.

The most famous building here is the "Red House". The predecessor of Zhijiang Campus, Zhijiang University, was one of the first Chinese higher education institutions designed by foreign architects. It was among the earliest to feature distinctly Western campus planning and design elements. Its buildings, constructed with unplastered red brick walls, seamlessly blend modern Western and traditional Oriental styles. The most striking building is the symmetrical red bell tower, with the entire structure resembling the Chinese character "山" ("mountain"). The bell tower, originally named Tonghuai Hall and also known as the Economics Hall, was built in 1936. It was donated by the family of Shi Liangcai, the manager of *Shenbao*, the most influential and longest-running commercial newspaper in Shanghai until 1949.

This red tower, tucked in the lush forest of Yuelun Hill, boasts both historical richness and conspicuousness. Many movies and TV dramas, such as *Aftershock*, *The Left Ear*, and *Decoded* have used this location for filming.

The beauty of Yuelun Hill cannot be fully appreciated through its well-known attractions alone, as its best scenery can only be captured from its top.

The hill itself is not tall, standing at only 153 meters above sea level, but the hike up is challenging. Starting from the Liuhe Pagoda Scenic Area, the trail takes you through Liaoqiao Hillock, Toulongtou Hill, Dahua Hill, Ma'er Hillock, and finally to

Guiren Pavilion at the hill behind Hupao Spring.

Yuelun Hill encompasses a vast expanse of forests. It takes about 2 hours to hike over the hills and hillocks to reach the hilltop.

The main entrance to the trail leading to Yuelun Hill is near Liuhetapailou Road, next to the ticket office for the Liuhe Pagoda Scenic Area. Most visitors head straight to Liuhe Pagoda, while very few take this side path. On the right side, near the public restroom, there is a walk, which is the hiking trail.

As you walk along this trail, you will find it stretching quietly into the distance. The path follows the spring of Yuelun Hill, which murmurs with clear and sweet waters. There are two "water-fetching points" beside the spring, where many local villagers often come with mineral water buckets to fill them with spring water.

If you walk about 500 meters further, you'll first see a tea garden nestled among lush trees and a memorial archway to its right. The archway leads to Gong Zhuiyu's tomb, a cultural relic protected at the provincial level.

Gong Zhuiyu, born in Hangzhou, was an official with numerous accomplishments during the Qing Dynasty. He held various positions, including Secretary in the Ministry of Household, Director in the Ministry of War, Surveillance Commissioner of Shandong Province, and Provincial Administrative Commissioner of Jiangnan. Throughout his life, he was promoted seven times. Emperor Kangxi appointed him to two chief positions simultaneously: Director of the Office of Imperial Sacrifices and Secretary of the Office of the Imperial Kitchen. He was one of the few officials who could hold two second-ranking positions, demonstrating the emperor's high regard for him.

Gong Zhuiyu lived up to the emperor's great expectations. During his over 30 years of service, he was honest and upright, just and law-abiding, and fearless of the privileged and influential. He made significant accomplishments in local governance and was highly esteemed and loved by the local people. He was also a renowned bibliophile during the early Qing Dynasty, known for his extensive knowledge and the tens of thousands of volumes he collected.

Gong Zhuiyu's tomb is one of the few well-preserved tombs of Qing Dynasty scholar-officials. The ornamental pillars, memorial archway, stele pavilions, stone horses, and stone tigers in front of the tomb remain intact, displaying great grandeur and majesty.

After passing Gong Zhuiyu's tomb, you will reach Liaoqiao Hillock. The slope there is gentle, and the stone steps are wide, making for an easy hike ahead.

To hike from Liaoqiao Hillock to Toulongtou Hill, you must climb countless winding steps that ascend steeply, presenting a significant challenge.

Thankfully, these steps are lined with green handrails, which can aid your ascent. However, the difficulty remains, especially for those who are not physically active in daily life. It takes a lot of courage to reach this point and continue climbing step by step.

Climbing these steps on hot days can probably be summed up by the popular Chinese phrase "choose to suffer". By the way, do you know how many steps there are in total? According to those who have reportedly counted them, there are either 666 or 686 steps.

After climbing the "666 steps"("666" literally means "good luck" in Chinese), you will reach a viewing spot where you can stand on an elevated rock and oversee the entire Qiantang River Bridge. The bridge and the river create a magnificent scene that unfolds before your eyes. It is truly a picturesque panorama!

The hill where you are standing is called Toulongtou Hill, and it is located northwest of Yuelun Hill. This is the starting point of the legendary "Jiulongtou" ("Nine Dragons' Heads"). The so-called "Jiulongtou" collectively refers to the hills in the area from the west of Liuhe Pagoda to Fancun Village and its surroundings along the Qiantang River. These hills are interconnected, undulating like dragons. Toulongtou Hill is the first of them, and the Zhijiang Campus of Zhejiang University is located on Erlongtou Hill, the second dragon's head.

When hiking from Toulongtou Hill through Dahua Hill to Ma'er Hillock, you will find the path easier to walk because it is smoother and gentler than the "666 steps". It is quite enjoyable to strain your eyes to take in the distant scenes, as the field of vision is very broad with no trees obstructing your view.

The best vantage point for sightseeing along the way is a boulder at the top of Dahua Hill, which offers a wide view and is an Instagrammable spot for many seasoned hikers.

Standing on the boulder, you can see the blue sky, white clouds, and rolling hills stretching as far as the eye can see. With such spectacular scenery before you, what worries could possibly trouble you? You'll instantly feel relaxed and at ease, regaining a bright mood.

But it is advised to be careful when taking pictures on the boulder. Do not go near its edge. One of its sides is marked with big red words "Caution:Fall Hazard".

This hiking route ends at Guiren Peak, located at the top of the hill behind Hupao Spring. Along the way, there are also diversions to Manjuelong, Jiuxi Creeks, and Li'an Temple.

The trail to the hill behind Hupao Spring still has endless steps, but thankfully, they are gently undulating and not too steep. Moreover, the lush hills and neatly arranged green tea fields will easily make you forget the fatigue of hiking.

Continue all the way to Guiren Peak on the rear hill of Hupao Spring, and you will find Guiren Pavilion at the top, which is another delightful surprise on Yuelun Hill.

This is an antiqued hexagonal pavilion with a double-eave roof, built in 2002. It stands 11.5 meters tall and features a spiral staircase in the middle. You can climb up to enjoy the view from the top. From here, with a 360-degree unobstructed view, you can simultaneously overlook West Lake, both banks of the Qiantang River, Yuhuang Hill, and the Northern and Southern Peaks, among other mountains. The view is truly excellent.

If you don't want to turn back, there are two other walking paths down from Guiren Pavilion. One is short but has steep stone steps, requiring you to take extra care while walking it; while the other is a bit longer but relatively gentle. Both paths lead to Hupao Park.

六和塔牌楼路
Liuhetapailou Road

六和塔往九溪、虎跑登山方向小径
230 The Path Leading to Jiuxi Creeks and Hupao Spring

远眺贵人阁
A View of Guiren Pavilion from a Distance

责任编辑　朱羽弘
文字编辑　乐文蔚
封面设计　巢倩慧　张瀛
责任校对　高余朵
责任印制　陈震宇

图书在版编目（CIP）数据

杭州Discovery. 再西湖 / 杭州西湖风景名胜区管理
委员会，都市快报编. -- 杭州 ： 浙江摄影出版社，
2025. 4. -- ISBN 978-7-5514-5212-0

Ⅰ. K928.955.1

中国国家版本馆CIP数据核字第20248ZD169号

Hangzhou Discovery·Zai Xihu

杭州Discovery·再西湖

杭州西湖风景名胜区管理委员会　编
都　市　快　报

全国百佳图书出版单位

浙江摄影出版社出版发行

　　地　址：杭州市环城北路 177 号
　　邮　编：310005
　　电　话：0571-85151082
网　址：www.photo.zjcb.com
制　版：浙江新华图文制作有限公司
印　刷：杭州捷派印务有限公司
开　本：710mm×1000mm　1/16
印　张：15.25
字　数：200千
2025年4月第1版 2025年4月第1次印刷
ISBN 978-7-5514-5212-0
定　价：68.00元